Witch-HUNT

MYSTERIES OF
the salem
WITCH TRIALS

Witch-HUNT

MYSTERIES OF the salem WITCH TRIALS

Marc Aronson

ATHENEUM BOOKS FOR YOUNG READERS
New York London Toronto Sydney

Atheneum Books for Young Readers

An imprint of Simon & Schuster Children's Publishing Division

1230 Avenue of the Americas

New York, New York 10020

Text copyright © 2003 by Marc Aronson

Chapter opener illustrations copyright © 2003 by Stephanie Anderson

Book design by Ann Bobco and Christopher Grassi

The text for this book is set in MrsEavesRoman.

Printed in the United States of America

First Edition

10 9 8 7 6 5 4 3 2 1

Library of Congress Cataloging-in-Publication Data

Aronson, Marc.

Witch-hunt : mysteries of the Salem witch trials / Marc Aronson.

v.   cm.

Includes bibliographical referencees.

Contents: Two Salem families, 1641–1692—Two mysteries—The mysteries end and the hearings begin—
The accuser: Ann Putnam, junior—The one and the many—From hearings to trials—The man in
black—Choosing death with a quiet conscience—That no more innocent blood be shed—A great
delusion of Satan.

ISBN 0-689-84864-1

1. Trials (Witchcraft)—Massachusetts—Salem—History—17th century—Juvenile literature. [1. Trials
(Witchcraft)—Massachusetts—Salem. 2. Witchcraft—Massachusetts—Salem. 3. Salem (Mass.)—
History—Colonial period, ca. 1600–1775.] I. Title.

KFM2478.8.W5 A76 2003

133.4'3'097445—dc21   2002152768

Photo Credits

American Antiquarian Society: p. 24

Barbados Archives: pp. 64, 65

Danvers Archival Center: pp. 7, 131 (both)

Houghton Library, Harvard University: p. 36 (all)

Lisa Aronson: p. 220

Massachusetts Archives: part title openers, p. 23

Massachusetts Historical Society: pp. 53, 182

Peabody Essex Museum (17,717 manuscript): p. 174

Richard B. Trask: p. 114

Robert Blair St. George's *Conversing By Signs: Poetics of
Implication in Colonial New England Culture.* (Chapel Hill, NC:
University of North Carolina Press, 1998.): p. 34 (both)

Selma Williams's *Riding the Nightmare: Women and Witchcraft
from the Old World to Colonial Salem.* (New York:
HarperPerennial, 1991.): p. 85

Winfield S. Nevins's *The Witches of Salem.* (Stamford, CT:
Longmeadow Press, 1994.): pp. 110, 146, 166, 168

To Noah, Milo, and Ruby, for reminding me always of my readers; to Alexander Ben Tarun Aronson, for the immeasurable increment of love he adds to our lives; and finally, to my mother, who reminded me when I began my research that she had worked on *The Crucible* with my father, making this a book that brings our family around full circle. I hope this book about families acting as agents of destruction is a record of a family finding, over the generations, new ways to create.

ACKNOWLEDGMENTS

I am grateful to Ginee Seo for suggesting this subject to me and for providing challenges and insights that helped me turn an accumulation of research and ideas into a book. George Nicholson was a most helpful adviser and guide in the mysteries of publishing. I have also been fortunate in receiving assistance from scholars. Professors Charles Cohen and Randall Balmer provided useful bibliographic leads, as did André Carus. Professor Bernard Rosenthal read the entire manuscript carefully, was gracious in his comments, and saved me from a number of errors.

It was my great good fortune to be able to read an early copy of Mary Beth Norton's landmark new study of Salem, *In the Devil's Snare,* just as my book went into production. As readers of the text and notes will see, I was able to enrich my narrative with her new insights, and, on two important points where I had not followed Professor Rosenthal's advice, her better example allowed me to recognize the folly of my ways. She was generous, too, in saving me from a number of small and foolish errors. But to get a full sense of her fresh approach and new interpretations, I urge my readers to go on to read her pathbreaking book. Finally, Richard Trask, archivist at the Danvers Archival Center, who is so often helpful to scholars of Salem, generously gave me informed guidance on images. Of course, I am solely responsible for all the facts, conclusions, and remaining limitations in this book.

Ken and Alexis Krimstein were wonderful companions when I wrote this book, and their recording of the late Nina Simone singing "Sinnerman" probably provided whatever narrative gusto is in the text. Shirley Budhos's loving attention to my son gave me great freedom to write. Marina, as ever, was the very best of readers: questioning, engaged, demanding only the best. There is probably no better way to become a writer than to be married to one who is constantly challenging herself and setting a high standard for the family.

CONTENTS:

Note to the Reader

As you will see, there are many different ways to interpret the witchcraft trials that took place in Salem, Massachusetts, in 1692. But there is one thing you can be sure of: If you have previously read novels for younger readers or popular adult accounts about those fascinating and frightening times, or if you have visited Salem itself, a good part of what you know is wrong. Over the centuries the actual events that took place that year were surrounded with a series of stories based on misinterpretations, fantasies, and half-truths that were passed along so many times from book to book that eventually they were treated as true.

For example, in one frequently told story the outbreak of witchcraft accusations begins when a black, or half-black, slave named Tituba teaches her Caribbean voodoo-inspired magic to local girls. Another staple scene of books on Salem opens with a couple of girls using occult methods to divine their future husbands' professions. When the experiment produces a ghastly result, the girls are terrified, and their strange symptoms set off all the witchcraft accusations. We read of satanic rituals in the woods, reminiscent to us now of scary practices in horror movies or of the allegedly ancient pagan practices that some claim to be reviving today. On the other side of the equation, the Puritan ministers, especially Cotton Mather, are often portrayed as driven, harsh inquisitors bent on oppressing women and stamping out any sign of spontaneous, life-affirming fun. Arthur Miller's play *The Crucible* combines many of these themes in a vividly rendered narrative. In his drama the events in Salem are explained as arising from a fear of sexuality, a willingness to give in to powerful families, and a tendency to demonize enemies.

In fact, Tituba was certainly an Indian, not African, and there is absolutely no evidence that she made use of any rituals of her own. If she practiced any "magic" at all, she used techniques she learned from the English. It is far from clear that the girls who were first afflicted were trying to figure out who their husbands would be through the old English practice of dropping an egg white in water and studying the shapes. Carefully read, the one record that perhaps indicates that a girl was spooked by seeing the image of a coffin in the water turns out to be a muddled blending of different stories.

Many people in New England believed in and used charms, astrological charts, and rituals handed down through the centuries to fend off evil influences, foretell the future, or interpret God's will. Though there is only very fragmentary evidence of this, it is not completely impossible that some even thought of themselves as witches. But there is no connection between these examples of folk magic and the modern practice of Wicca. The Puritan ministers, including Mather, were much more measured and troubled in their response than legend would have it. *The Crucible* is a psychologically astute historical drama that is quite useful for understanding the 1950s in which it was written, but it is no guide to making sense of events in the 1690s.

For decades scholars have tried to clear away this underbrush and to make sense of what the original sources actually tell us. I am the beneficiary of their diligence and have been inspired to make a few corrections of my own. You can see the trail of historical detective work in the "Notes and Comments" section at the back of this book.

If you would like to learn more about the events of 1692 by visiting modern Salem, you will see the traces of the very stories scholars no longer accept. You can learn of supposedly real witches and visit amusement park–style haunted houses. These venues either offer some fun and scary thrills or "honor" the witches of the past by recognizing them as believers in a kind of alternative, female-oriented nature religion. Other reenactments tell the anti-Puritan version of the Salem story, depicting replicas of the dungeons of the day or reading from actual transcripts, to show how mean and cruel the judges and ministers were. These exhibits and performances are more or less entertaining, but they are not very helpful in understanding the past.

We can say what did *not* happen at Salem. It is much harder to say what did. The challenge of this book is to

give you enough information to begin to think that
through for yourself. If the study of the witchcraft
accusations, and of the mythologies that have grown up
around them, teaches anything, it is that we must be
careful with evidence. But caution is not the same as
resignation. We are not likely to ever know, with certainty, why the events at Salem unfolded as they did.
Yet looking for new clues about Salem, re-examining
old ones, formulating theories, and testing them is
ever the more fascinating just because it is an ongoing
process. Being careful not to recycle false stories, you
just may arrive at the one that is closest to being true.

Precisely because the most diligent scholarship will
probably never be able to "solve" all the mysteries of
Salem, there is room for your imagination. At the heart
of the whole story is one central question: Why did the
accusers do it? Why did they twitch and scream and
bleed in court? Why did they cause nineteen people to
be hanged and a total of perhaps twenty-five to die?
Many of the accusers were teenagers. I hope that when
you reach this question again, in Chapter X, you will
have enough historical context to use your own experience, your own sense of yourself as a modern teenager,
to try to picture them, your ancestors centuries ago. A
group of individuals acted as a pack to attack and
destroy others. Is that because they were in such a dis-
tressed state of mind that they actually believed their
neighbors were agents of evil? If so, what horrors, real
or imagined, could have driven them to that state? Or

is it that the attackers themselves knowingly acted in evil ways? If they did, why did they? And why were some able to resist?

In one way, the accusers were products of their time and were very different from you. This book, and the notes in the back, will give you the chance to see how different they were. But in another sense your knowledge of yourself does give you a way to begin envisioning and imagining them. And the great joy of history is that as long as we are careful with evidence, we have the power to constantly re-create the past in our minds. I hope you will join me in that process. Perhaps you will discover something about Salem none of us have so far been able to see.

⊰ ✴ ⊱

A Note About the Images in This Book

The only images that have survived from the period are of a few of the most famous judges and ministers, and only one building is still standing in Salem. Any paintings readers may have seen in other books were done in the nineteenth century, and while they may have been generally accurate we know almost nothing about what the accusers and the accused looked like. This means that any book about Salem will either include new art, or have only text pages.

On Spelling, Word Usage, and Dates in This Book

I have not used the original spelling or punctuation in the transcripts of the pretrial hearings, which are the main source we have about the events. Here is a typical line: "And further I heard him tell Jeams bridges . . . that he loved a gurll at fourteen years ould: which: said bridges: oned to be the truth." (Modern-day translation: "And further, I heard him tell James Bridges . . . that he loved a fourteen-year-old girl, which that same Bridges owned [admitted] to be the truth.") There is a certain pleasure in decoding this writing, but for the purposes of clarity, I have modernized the spelling and punctuation.

I have chosen to use the term *Indian* rather than *Native American* for a variety of reasons. For one, *The British Museum Encyclopedia of Native North America,* by Rayna Green (director of the American Indian Program, National Museum of American History, Smithsonian Institution) and Melanie Fernandez (acting first nations officer at the Ontario Art Council), explains that "most American Indians prefer to refer to their tribal names, using the general term 'Indian' and, more rarely, 'Native American' in everyday speech" (p. 109). This accords with what I have heard from other experts. I do not believe there is a truly "correct" term now, and it would be anachronistic to use a modern phrase for seventeenth-century peoples. For another, using *Native American* would lead to a hopeless muddle when referring to Tituba, an Indian from Barbados, who may or may not have had North American Indian roots. She was native and American but probably not Native American in the modern sense, and the same applies to her husband, who was named John Indian.

The New Englanders of the time still used the Julian calendar. They refused to accept the Gregorian calendar, in part because it had been approved by the pope. That meant they considered New Year's Day to be March 25, and thus all dates in January, February, and most of March were from the previous year. So March 1, 1692—a very important date in the story—is written in documents of the time as either March 1, 1691, or March 1, 1691/2. I have written all dates in modern form. As long as you know the general rule, you should be able to make sense of original sources even when their dating seems to differ from mine by a year.

Of dark forests and Midnight Thoughts

s for our Sov[n] Lord and Lady the Kin[g]
That Sarah Buckley Wife of Willia[m]

In the County of Essex Shoom[?]
[th]e Eighteenth day of May

aforesaid and divers other days an[d]
as after Certaine detestable Arts
ous[?] Wickedly Mallitiously and fell[oniously]
[us]ed and Exercised At and in the Tow[n]
[Coun]ty of Essex aforesaid in u[pon?]
[Pu]ttman of Salem

[by] which
[Joh]n Puttman y Day & Year[?] afor[esaid]
[a]nd times both before and after [was?]
[affl]icted Consumed Pined Wasted & [Tormented?]
[su]ndry other Acts of Witchcraft by [the said Sarah]
[Buc]kley Contrarie done before a[nd]
[again]st Our Sov[n] Lord and Lady the [King]
[Cr]owne & Dignity and the forme[r]

"The QUEEN of hell"

May 31, 1692   *In a plain Salem meetinghouse a woman stands before her judges. The magistrate—we are not sure if it was John Hathorne or Jonathan Corwin—speaks with the stern, suspicious voice of the community. The accusers, girls and young women, are fervent, overexcited, just on the edge of breaking into convulsions. They are so tormented, it is as if their very bones are being pulled out of their sockets.*

Judge: Abigail Williams, who hurts you?
Abigail Williams: Goody Carrier of Andover.
Judge: Elizabeth Hubbard, who hurts you?

ELIZABETH HUBBARD: Goody Carrier.

JUDGE: Susannah Sheldon, who hurts you?

SUSANNAH SHELDON: Goody Carrier. She bites me, pinches me, and tells me she would cut my throat, if I did [do] not sign her book.

The accused is a poor, unpopular woman from Andover, who had her first child before she was married. She is also suspected of having spread smallpox and has spoken sharply to her neighbors. No wonder she is called "Goody" (Goodwife); only married women of high status are called "Mrs." But she is unrelenting in maintaining her innocence.

JUDGE: What do you say to this you are charged with?

MARTHA CARRIER: I have not done it.

Susannah cries out, saying she can see an evil man or the devil himself, dressed in black. This evil specter appears many times and is called "the black man."
Ann Putnam Jr. suddenly feels a pin being stuck in her.

JUDGE: What black man is that?

MARTHA CARRIER: I know none.

Ann sees the man; she insists he is here in the room. And Mary Warren takes up Ann's part; she is feeling something piercing her skin.

JUDGE: What black man did you see?

MARTHA CARRIER: I saw no black man but your
own presence.

*The girls are beginning to wail now, baring their wounds, hold-
ing out the very real pins that draw their blood, collapsing as if struck
down by invisible rays blazing from Martha's eyes. The judge believes
the young women are under demonic attack and uses their agonies
to press Martha to confess her own sin. But Martha, stoic, almost
disdainful in her calm disgust, sees only lies.*

JUDGE: Can you look upon these and not knock
them down?

MARTHA CARRIER: They will dissemble if I look
upon them.

JUDGE: You see you look upon them and they fall
down.

MARTHA CARRIER: It is false; the Devil is a liar. I
looked at no one since I came into the room but
you.

*Standoff: The unswerving judge, the unbending accused. And
now the accusers ratchet up the emotions another notch.*

*Susan has fallen into a kind of trance, and she sees ghosts
materialize in the room.*

SUSANNAH SHELDON: I wonder what [how many]
could you murder, thirteen persons?

*Mary Walcott can see the dead spirits too, thirteen ghosts
hovering in the air. And now all the afflicted people scream and
howl. Elizabeth and Ann go beyond claiming to see ghosts; they tell
the court that they are sure that Martha killed thirteen people in
Andover.*

MARTHA CARRIER: It is a shameful thing that you
should mind [take seriously] these folks that are
out of their wits.
JUDGE: Do you not see them?
MARTHA CARRIER: If I do speak, you will not
believe me [will you]?

The accusers insist that Martha, too, can see the ghosts.

MARTHA CARRIER: You lie. I am wronged.

*Mercy Lewis falls into a violent fit, as if driven mad by
Martha's opposition. By this point, the court record tells us, "the
torture of the afflicted was so great that there was no enduring of
it, so that she [Martha] was ordered away and to be bound hand
and foot. . . . The afflicted meanwhile [were] almost killed."*

How could such a scene take place in a legal hearing?
How could solemn, thoughtful, rational men have taken
seriously the screams of accusers whose visions were never
scrutinized? How could these same judges ignore the sober
honesty of the accused? A leading minister later described
Martha as a "rampant hag" who had been promised that she

would be made queen of hell by the devil himself. This seems so unlike the Martha who appears in the transcripts that the minister appears to be writing about a different person. But he wasn't; the difference is in our perception of her, which leads us to the next question: Why would young people join together to attack someone they had hardly, if ever, met, knowing their wails and visions and fits would lead to her death?

In order to begin answering these questions, we have to step outside the courtroom, into the world of fairy tales.

Though there is nothing left of the original building, this is the site of the meetinghouse in which the first accused witches were questioned.

Two FAMILIAR FAIRY tales

Think back to the stories you read or heard as a child: tales in which fairy godmothers offer servant girls wonderful clothes so they can attend grand balls; in which villagers wander off the road into the dark forest and are lost to wolves and monsters that lurk in the shadows; in which malicious old women cast spells and confer with their evil black cats; in which foolish or greedy farmers sign pacts with a strangely elegant man, catching sight of his cloven hoof or trailing tail or getting a whiff of sulfur only when it is too late.

Now imagine what the world would feel like if these were not charming old fables, but true. Martha Carrier's own eight-year-old daughter described just such a world to Judge Hathorne. Sarah Carrier was sweet-tempered, easy to talk to, and certain she had been a witch ever since she was six years old. She had been converted by her mother, she said, who lured her into touching the red book with the white pages. Martha appeared to her as a cat, one that could terrify her by threatening to tear her to pieces but one that could also wing her spirit away over the treetops to attack others.

What if, like Sarah, you knew as sure as the sun would rise in the morning that witches lived among you and could bring pain, even death, to you, your defenseless babies, your precious livestock and crops? What we call "fairy tales" are often simply the record of the world as many of our ancestors experienced it. Evil spirits, and the witches who courted them, supplied causes for events that were otherwise inexplicable. Witches were conduits of harm who brought pain and suffering into people's lives. They offered a very concrete and emotionally appealing explanation for the often perplexing and painful twists and turns of life. Read a fairy tale carefully, and you can see the logic behind the witchcraft trials.

Take the story of Sleeping Beauty. Once upon a time, the story begins, there was a royal couple unable to have children. When they finally do have a daughter and hold a grand celebration, they slight one old woman while giving gifts to all the others. The old woman's fury, her anger at not getting her due, makes her decide to kill—or permanently put to sleep—the beautiful baby.

Anyone who reads the fairy tale today is sure to care about the child. We want the old woman to be prevented from doing her evil deeds, maybe even killed. We are reacting in exactly the same way as did villagers who, for hundreds of years, condemned witches. After all, the story leaves out two big questions: Why did the king and queen slight the old woman, and how were they able finally to have a child? One way to answer these questions is to see the old woman as a midwife, a wisewoman, the one who made Sleeping Beauty's birth possible. Another is to picture her as an unpopular, perhaps unattractive and bitter old woman, whom it was easy to ignore. In either case, how did the royal couple, the "good guys," repay the woman who answered their prayers (in version one) or the poor outsider who was envious of their good fortune (in version two)? By ignoring her, slighting her, and then, when she shows her anger, by destroying her. And we cheer them on.

Studies of the witchcraft cases in sixteenth- and seventeenth-century England for which court records have survived show that about 80 percent of those accused were women. Though the term *witch* applied equally to men and women, women wound up in court four times as often. One historian's analysis of the 114 witchcraft cases in New England in the seventeenth century (not including the Salem episode) shows that, again, at least 80 percent of those formally charged with being witches were women. The more closely historians have looked at these records, the more clearly they have seen stories much like the beginning of Sleeping Beauty: a man or woman who was owed something and didn't get it; a woman whom people depended on for medical help but thus also feared; a man or woman who had suffered losses and who then turned angry and vengeful, was very likely to be called a witch.

From the point of view of people in the farms and small villages of England and New England, a witch tended to be someone who did not fit in. She was a woman who had few or no children, or was past her childbearing years, and yet owned property. She was a person, in other words, who lived outside the pattern of life people expected of a woman, in which her role and her assets were devoted to her family. And she was especially suspect if she was outspoken, not modest and quiet. A man or woman who was bitter, who was angry, who disrupted the harmony of daily life was the very image of a witch.

This was all the more true if the person had a reason to be angry. Accusers often saw evidence of witchcraft in people whom they had refused to help. As in the story of Sleeping Beauty, the frustration, anger, and envy of the outsider only made those who had rejected that person think it was more likely that he or she would turn outside the community for aid. And who better to help bitter people to get revenge than Satan, the Prince of Darkness, the angel whose own envy of God made him try to subvert all of creation?

Sleeping Beauty shows how readily we side with witchcraft accusers. Another story, that of Cinderella, helps explain why our ancestors felt so troubled by seductive spirits. That familiar tale tells of a servant girl who is really suited to be the bride of a prince but who is forced into harsh labor by her evil stepmother, until she is saved by a fairy godmother who is able to give her magical entry into a royal ball. Here is how a very similar story, changed just slightly, actually took place in 1671.

It might well have been one of those gray, cold New England days when the chill gets into your bones and layers of homespun do little to keep it out. The sky on those days is filled with clouds, and the sun's light is pale and thin. It is a cruel tease, promising warmth it never delivers. At any moment a wind gust can bully you, telling you that coldness is in charge here, winter is the rule. Suddenly, everything in your own life feels as bare, stony, and harsh as the landscape around you.

Perhaps it was on a day such as this that Elizabeth Knapp, a teenage girl from a troubled family, was doing chores. She was now a servant, working for the Reverend Samuel Willard and staying in his home. The reverend was a learned man, much respected, and nothing like Elizabeth's own father, who often ran afoul of the law. Perhaps he seemed like a savior to Elizabeth, a good strong man who was everything her undependable father was not. He gave her work and a roof over her head. But in a way, he, too, was unreliable, for he was often away, and she was left alone on those gray New England days, endlessly sweeping and hauling, cleaning and cooking, being useful and silent.

Suddenly, a voice spoke to Elizabeth in her mind. It was a grand voice—as grand as the Reverend Willard's—but it was evil. The devil offered to relieve her of one of her chores by taking in the wood chips she still had to bring in for the family fire. Elizabeth refused. But when she came into the house, she saw the chips already there. Elizabeth was terrified. What had she done? Had her resentment and envy let the devil in? Had she already made a pact, signed her name in his book in blood? Was she lost and damned? Elizabeth was haunted by her discontentment, by the voice she heard in the shadows, by the devil, who seemed to loom so close to her inmost thoughts. How

far is this scenario of a strange dark man saving a servant girl from her chores from that of Cinderella's
fairy godmother turning a pumpkin into a coach?
Once again, behind a familiar fairy tale is the world of
witches.

Listen now to another one of Martha Carrier's
accusers, twelve-year-old Phoebe Chandler. Phoebe's
mother asked her to fetch some beer to slake the thirst
of nearby workers. As Phoebe neared the fence to the
lot they were in, she heard "a voice in the bushes
(which I thought was Martha Carrier's voice, which I
know well) but saw nobody, and the voice asked me
what I did [was doing] there and whether [where] I was
going, which greatly frightened me, so that I ran as fast
as I could to those at work."

Phoebe escaped, but when her mother sent her
back a few hours later on another chore, "I heard the
same voice, as I judged, over my head, saying I should
[would] be poisoned within two or three days, which
accordingly happened, as I conceive, for I went to my
sister Allen's farm the same day; on Friday following,
about one half of my right hand was greatly swollen and
exceeding painful."

A walk in the sunshine for Phoebe was like the plot
of a horror film for us. In every clump of grass lurked
the mysterious voice of an angry neighbor, who might
be an agent of the devil and who had the power to make
her sick if she did not obey. Phoebe was not an excep-
tionally overimaginative girl. Nor was Benjamin

Abbot, a grown man who had very similar experiences. When he got into an argument over some land with Martha Carrier, she seemed to curse him by warning that she would stick as close to him as bark to a tree. All of sudden he began to suffer mysterious ailments, including a swollen foot and a running sore, which disappeared once Martha was arrested.

If your daily experience includes curses that come true, it makes perfect sense that your friends are haunted by ghosts in a courtroom and are attacked by evil spirits that only they can see. Much of what we know about such beliefs comes from the court records of witchcraft trials, which are imperfect sources. People often speak very carefully when their words result in winning or losing a case. The transcripts were taken down by individual friends of the court, not official recorders, and were not meant to be word-for-word accounts. Many have been lost. But court records and fairy tales are not the only ways to peer back into the collective of such accusers as Sarah Carrier, Elizabeth Knapp, Phoebe Chandler, and Benjamin Abbot.

Skittering
SHADOWS How do we explain the inexplicable today? We are told by people we respect that microscopic germs and viruses cause disease, that vast high- and low-pressure systems stretching across the globe create local weather patterns, and that ribbons of nearly invisible genetic material determine what color

eyes our children will have; but few of us have actually done experiments to test these ideas or have even carefully read the studies conducted by others. We accept these theories, which do not match what we see with our own eyes, on faith. In the seventeenth century most people accepted on faith a very different understanding of how the invisible world interacted with daily life. They believed that God ultimately judged and determined everything—that was the single clearest "cause" for any effect seen in the world. But many also believed that there were other invisible forces, good and bad, present in their lives. And so do we, even now.

When a dark shadow skitters across the floor, how sure are you of what you saw or did not see out of the corner of your eye? When you know someone envies you or has reason to resent you, and you see that person stare at you and then you suddenly experience a strange pain, don't you wonder if that person somehow managed to make you suffer? When you want something with all your heart, don't you wish rituals or ceremonies designed to invoke the aid of spirits might help you? Don't you test out what kinds of deals you would be willing to make with anyone or anything to get your way? And then don't you worry about what you might have given away? When you or someone you love has a setback, don't you ask yourself, *Is it something I did?* and then try to solve the problem by changing your life? When someone you know is really, really, really upset—

scary, frightening, out of control, in tears, rage, wildness—can you tell whether that person is faking it or in a true crisis or in some weird state you don't understand? When our nation is attacked, don't you walk more fearfully, want to destroy our enemies, and have a clear and preset image of who they may be?

The world of the Salem witches is in one sense long ago and far away. But in another sense, it is the world as we experience it at dusk, when dark shadows make everything seem eerie, or when we are up alone late at night, or anytime when we are not participating in the common world we share with parents and teachers, friends and relations. If you begin reading about the seventeenth century with those moments in your mind, it is not so distant at all. No matter what we say on tests and in public, in private we often explain the world the same way our ancestors did. And yet there are no longer court cases in the United States in which you can be tried for being a witch. So something has changed dramatically from then to now. We have driven the monsters into our private thoughts and onto the faces of our political opponents. They are no longer out there as a supernatural force. The Salem witch trials are the record of that transition.

BELIEF
or FRAUD? The fact that many people in seventeenth-century New England believed in witches, devils, spells, and amulets does not mean that everyone

did, and certainly not in every case. Throughout the 1600s, people came into New England's courts accusing their neighbors of being witches. Surprisingly, in most cases the judge or the jury ruled *against* the accusers or chose not to execute those who were convicted. This was not an expression of doubt about witchcraft itself, which both the law and common belief asserted was real. Rather, it was because witchcraft was a hard case to prove. Unlike courts on the European continent, those in England and New England would not accept evidence obtained by torture. Defenders of torture believed that getting the truth was so important, the court could use any means to obtain it. (This very argument was raised in the United States after the September 11, 2001, terrorist attacks.) English courts protected suspects against this treatment, but that made it harder to prove cases against them. In New England the courts went even a step further, by banning traditional "tests" to uncover witches. Suspects, for example, could not be dunked in water (with the idea that a real witch would float), as had often been done in England.

The higher bar for evidence matched a mood of suspicion in New England's courts. Even though nearly everyone agreed that witches really existed, when it came to making a legal judgment, those same believers had a canny eye for misguided people, disturbed people, people who were just using the courts to settle scores. One common way for an accused witch to fight back

was to bring his own lawsuit, claiming that the indictment was an insult and made him look bad in the eyes
of the community. Often enough, the accused won
these cases.

The Salem story is unusual—not because there were
claims of witchcraft, but because the courts believed
them from the first. Then the rules of evidence
seemed to change, probably allowing both physical and
psychological torture; Sarah Carrier's young brothers,
for instance, may well have been subjected to terrible
abuse in prison. Soon men joined women in being
accused, convicted, and executed in numbers that had
never been seen before in North America; and finally,
more and more people began to confess. What started
out as a relatively typical and minor case exploded
into a crisis. Explaining why that happened in 1692,
just eight decades before the American Revolution,
requires more than seeing into the minds of New
Englanders who heard the devil whispering to them on
dark nights. It also raises the sickening possibility that
cynical or angry or disturbed people used popular
ideas about the powers of evil for their own evil ends.

Perhaps the nineteen people who were executed by
hanging (an additional man was killed by being pressed
to death by heavy stones for refusing to make a plea,
and at least five other people, including two infants,
died in prison) were not the victims of the beliefs of
their time, but rather victims of one set of their neighbors who were willing, even eager, to participate in

legal murder and of another group too afraid to stop them. This very concern haunted many people at the time, from the greatest ministers and leaders to young servants and children. How they responded to this concern is the heart of the Salem story. For the mounting executions forced a people dedicated to living by God's laws to keep asking themselves whether they were enforcing those divine rules or abusing them. This was a great test for the New England Puritans, and it began in 1688, in Boston.

Boston, 1688: The Possession of the Goodwin Children

s for our So[vereign] Lord and La[dy] the K[ing]
That Sarah Buckley Wife of Willia[m]

In the County of Essex Shoom[aker]
[th]e Eighteenth day of May

aforesaid and divers other days an[d]
as after Certaine detestable Arts
[call]ed Witchery Malitiously and fel[oniously]
[use]d and Exercised At and in the To[wn]
[Coun]ty of Essex — Aforesaid in [one]
[Mercy Le]wisman of Salem

[upon]
[An]n Puttnam [the] Day & Yeare Afor[said]
[and] times both before and often w[as]
[aff]licted Consumed Pined Wasted & [tortured]
[su]ndry other Acts of Witchcraft by
[the said Buck]ley — Committed and done before
[again]st Our So[vereign] Lord and Lady the [King &]
[C]rowne & Dignity and the forme [of the statute]

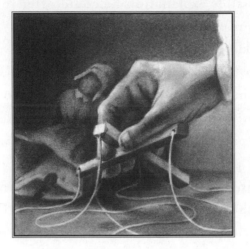

MATHER
vs GLOVER
The trouble began in the summer of 1688. Thirteen-year-old Martha Goodwin noticed that some of her family's linen was missing and sharply questioned their washerwoman, who she suspected had stolen it. The laundress's mother was furious and attacked Martha with terrible words. Goody Glover's "bad language" seemed to afflict Martha like a contagious disease. The girl, and soon her three younger siblings, fell into fits. These seemed so painful that the prominent minister who later wrote up the case reported that "it would have broke a heart of stone to have seen their agonies." When the

respected physician Thomas Oakes was called in, the
only possible explanation he could offer for the children's suffering was witchcraft.

Luckily, it was not hard to guess who was responsible for harming the Goodwin children. Glover—her
first name is not known for certain, though she is
often mistakenly called "Mary"—was made-to-order
for the part. An angry older woman, she was just the
sort of person whom people suspected of being a
witch. In fact, not six years earlier, as a woman lay
dying, she had revealed to another woman that Glover
had bewitched her to death. And just as the woman
who was carrying this secret was preparing to testify against the witch, her
son was assaulted by a "black
thing with a blue cap" that
appeared in his room to torment him. Though Glover
was just a poor woman, she
seemed able to cause great
harm by using the powers
of evil. Her imprisonment
immediately healed the youngest
of the Goodwin children, but when
she again railed at them,
the other three relapsed.

Cotton Mather was a young minister when he
came to the Goodwin household. He went on
to write many books and became a leading
authority on Puritanism in Massachusetts.

To face off against
Glover and the devil—the evil one who surely was
responsible for the anguish Glover was causing the

Goodwin children—a young but important minister arrived at the household. He was Cotton Mather—son of Increase Mather, one of the leading ministers and theologians of his day, and grandson of John Cotton, one of the most important ministers and authors in the early history of New England. In his lineage, his already impressive learning, and his presence, Cotton Mather was the ideal person to aid the Goodwin children. If he could entrap Glover and get her to reveal her satanic bond, he could free the young people from her malign influence.

Mather, already in Boston, arrived at their home to try to help four children who lived near the church in which he preached. But he was also there to participate in what he knew was a far larger and more momentous cause. This case was both a test and a potential rallying point for all of New England Puritans.

Of MEETINGHOUSES and the
blood of WOLVES:
the PURITAN journey The Puritans' mission in
America was clearest in the early days of their New England settlements. The Puritans had arrived on ships. Built of long wooden planks, their churches were like simple wooden boats on land, safeguarding the believers inside. And, as one of their descendants, Nathaniel Hawthorne, wrote, when one of them killed a wolf, he claimed his reward by nailing it "on the porch of the meetinghouse," where the blood would drip onto

the doorstep. This balance of simple strength and fierce combat was the essence of Puritanism.

Puritans turned completely away from what they saw as the old props of religion. Rich cathedrals full of statues, stained-glass images, ceremonies where the scent of incense or the sound of ancient chants might set the mood, priests speaking in a foreign language—all had no place in their religion. Instead, they built their faith on clean, simple planks, like the timber of their churches, on the Word of God as written in the Bible, translated into English, and shared by the congregation.

The Puritans, or "the Godly" as they were often called in England, were pleased with their spare, simple churches with their hard wooden benches. Religion for them was not a moment here or there—a sermon on the Sabbath Day, a prayer at meals, pious phrases on holy days. Nor were they called "Puritans" because they wanted a pure, clear faith filling every part of life and every moment of every day. Each household was considered a little congregation, with the father as a kind of minister. He would lead the family in prayer and Bible reading, and he would discipline those who needed it. Children were viewed as prideful and stubborn. Their early education involved breaking them of that willfulness and making them more humble and obedient. While in some ways this was a very severe kind of family life, Puritans thought of it as based on love. They believed that husbands and wives should love each other, passionately and intimately. And the harsh treatment of young children only made sense since it gave them the best chance of discovering God's love, which was the greatest gift of all.

The Puritans believed that each person was on the most difficult, dangerous, and uncertain path: the journey toward God. In England they had to struggle against the government even to practice their faith. Their absolute devotion to religion as they understood it, their unwillingness to accept compromise, and their hatred of Catholics clashed with the policies of English kings content with an easier faith that asked less of people. Faced with this kind of opposition in 1603, King James I warned that he would chase them out of the country. But this persecution only strengthened their faith. Puritans who crossed the sea and arrived in New England felt they were participating in a new kind of pilgrimage, the physical epic of starting over in a new land. And the physical was linked to the spiritual growth. Every tree felled, field planted, simple meetinghouse built was a step in the creation of the kingdom of the Lord.

The Puritans were a minority among the English settlers in New England, and from the first, they had conflicts with others who came to North America only to make money or to live according to their own rules. But their sense of what crossing the ocean meant was very influential. Anyone today who feels that Americans have a special destiny as a force for religious faith or

democracy or economic opportunity is sharing in and
carrying on the Puritans' vision of this land.

Devout Puritans interpreted everything that happened to them on their pilgrimage in the new land—
epidemics of illness, wars with Indians, the sickness or
health of their families, earthquakes, even the severity
of New England winters—as judgments of their behavior. They saw themselves as living out the story of the
Jews, the chosen people in the Bible, who had to wander in the wilderness after they left Egypt. The stark
meetinghouse colored with the blood of a wolf was the
modern version of the tents of the Jews, carrying the
Word of the Lord to the Promised Land.

Puritans drew great strength from seeing themselves
in combat with the world around them. In their wars
against the Indians, for example, they could be completely and coldly destructive. For a time they offered
bounties for the scalps of murdered Indians. In this
sense they were like those fundamentalists of all reli-
gions today who can justify extreme measures against
others—whether that be attacking U.S. cities, killing
doctors who perform abortions, or settling in occupied
territories—on the grounds that they have a divine right
to take them. They considered themselves an outpost of
saints in a hostile wilderness. Any victory against their
foes seemed to prove the rightness of their mission; any
defeat was a sign of God's dissatisfaction.

Seeing themselves as a spiritual community,
Puritans especially feared being attacked by the devil,

the enemy of God. Those who rejected God entirely and made pacts with the devil were, in the eyes of Puritan believers, a combination of our worst fears of spies and terrorists. Since you could not immediately recognize these traitors, they could pass as the most pious of churchgoing neighbors—which meant you constantly had to be on guard. Anyone who yearned for a simpler, easier way to happiness could be tempted. According to one woman who confessed to being a witch during the Salem trials, the devil promised her, "We should have happy days and then it would be better times for me." The devil felt equally present to people who thought they were failing God. Like Elizabeth Knapp, they feared they had lost their souls already.

Witchcraft and prayer actually had something very important in common. If the devil was lurking nearby, turning people into witches, then God was equally close at hand, saving souls. The threat of one proved the existence of the other. This equation was very important to Cotton Mather when he came to help the Goodwin children, for on every front the mission that had brought his family to New England was under assault.

Four years before, in 1684, the frighteningly pro-Catholic Charles II had dissolved the original charter of the Massachusetts Bay Colony, which had allowed the Puritan leaders to govern as they saw fit. New England was now being run by an arrogant Englishman named Sir Edmond Andros. Andros was questioning whether long-established farmers really owned their land. Worse, he was insisting that any Christian could come into the community. That meant that Quakers had to be tolerated. All good Puritans knew that Quakers trembled and shook in their meetings and claimed to be in touch with an inner light. To the Godly, this sounded suspiciously like possession. Puritans were being told to allow people who might be directly in touch with the devil into their towns and villages.

Outside New England's borders the news was equally frightening. King Philip's War, a ferocious conflict with the Indians a decade earlier, had led to extremes of death and suffering on both sides. Though unprecedented killing and cruelty allowed the New Englanders to win, the war left scars: disabled men, lost relatives, and the certainty that remaining Indians could see their neighbors only as mortal enemies. Farther north, the Catholic French and their Indian allies were a constant threat. In order to help people picture the danger witchcraft posed, Cotton Mather described the devils themselves as something very like those Catholics. Think of them, he urged, as "vast regiments of cruel and bloody French dragoons [soldiers], with an Intendant [general] over them, overrunning a pillaged neighborhood."

Despite these very serious threats, young people did not seem to need the church in the same ways as their parents. And even those in the older generation paled in comparison to their forebears, who had

braved the unknown in an effort to create a model
society in a new land. For Cotton Mather, a tangle with
a witch was an opportunity to remind everyone in New
England of why they were there: They were participants
in a great battle, a cosmic struggle as in biblical times,
and they could never take their enemy, the true enemy
of God, too lightly.

Testing
a WITCH
What was a witch? It depended
upon whom you asked. On the popular level, judging
by the way people told stories and eyed their neighbors and brought cases to court, a witch was a person
who could do harm through magical means. A witch,
male or female, could curdle milk, hobble animals,
and even cause young children to sicken and die.
There were many folkways that told people how to
figure out if someone was a witch, and how to combat one who had been flushed out. For example, one
English folk belief held that if a child or baby was
passed through a hole in a natural object such as a
rock or a tree, that child would be immune to witchcraft. Apparently, there was a tree in Salem that had
a gap of just the right size, and parents continued to
pass their babies through it long after the trials. The
last recorded case of using the tree this way took place
on July 8, 1793.

Some of the methods for telling the future, doing
harm to others, and detecting malign forces were part

of what Mather called "little sorceries" but which we would no longer call "witchcraft." The year before the Salem outbreak, Mather lamented that "in some towns it has been a usual thing for people to cure hurts with spells, or to use detestable conjurations, with sieves, keys, and peas, and nails, and horseshoes, and I know not what other implements to learn the things for which they have a forbidden, and an impious curiosity. 'Tis in the Devil's name that such things are done."

The rituals Mather cited were the seventeenth-century equivalent of such diversions as checking your horoscope in the daily paper, hunting for four-leaf-clovers, or consulting a Ouija board. For instance, according to a late-sixteenth-century English manuscript, the sieve and scissors were used this way: "Stick a pair of shears [scissors] in the rind [handle] of a sieve and let two persons set the top of each of their forefingers upon the upper part of the shears holding it with the sieve up from the ground steadily; ask Peter and Paul whether A, B, or C hath stolen the thing lost; and at the nomination of the guilty person the sieve will turn around."

English settlers brought these practices with them across the Atlantic, but Mather and other leading ministers were trying to eliminate them. On the one hand, they thought these games were dangerous, for they toyed with using the devil's own powers, even if they were not used for devilish ends. The ministers saw no distinction between "white" and "black" magic. The only nonhuman power a person should rely on, they believed, was God. On the other hand, the ministers saw themselves as men of reason who relied on experiment and knowledge, not superstition. To them, spiritual matters were a type of science. Dealing with evidence of the occult required the very same rationality and discipline applied to navigating across the seas or planning how to sow your crops. Folk magic had no place in their world.

To ministers such as Mather, as well as to the law of the day, a witch was a person who had made a pact with the devil. Claims of having been harmed by magic could be used to arouse suspicion about a person. But a witch could be convicted only by confessing or by the testimony of two or more witnesses who were sure they had seen evidence of the diabolical link.

Mather set out to get Glover to reveal who and what she was. At first he tried a simple test: He asked her to recite the Lord's Prayer. Many believed that being in league with the devil would make it impossible for a person to speak these holy words. Glover mangled line after line. This was the seventeenth-century equivalent of failing a lie detector test today, and she was quickly brought to trial. Suddenly, a complication arose. Glover claimed not to understand English, only Gaelic. This was possibly true, as Glover was from Ireland and was a Catholic. But through an interpreter, she confessed all. The court hurried to search her home, and

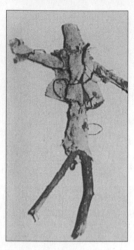

These seventeenth-century cloth puppets were found hidden in the walls of a home in Cutchogue, Long Island. The strange headless, sticklike figures look like objects used in rituals in many parts of the world.

damning evidence was found: "several small images, or puppets, or babies, made of rags, and stuffed with goat's hair." Everyone knew that witches used such props to hurt people from a distance.

The importance of puppets in witch trials suggests something of what witches meant to people at the time. A witch had given up her soul so that she could command Satan's power. In that sense she

was a puppet master. She could now use invisible forces to harm her victims. But by deadening her soul, she had also lost her humanity and made herself into a tool of evil. She was now a puppet herself. Either way, as powerful tormentor or as soulless pseudohuman, a witch was terrifying. Not only was she different in that she was a woman living an odd, inexplicable kind of life, not only was she a troublemaker because of her angry words and loud mouth, but a witch was the less-than-human more-than-human force in the village who was personally responsible for anything that went wrong. A witch subverted lives that should have been good. But that was only because God allowed her to do so, as a test of or a punishment for the faithful.

Despite having the crucial evidence found in Glover's home, the judges did not want to jump to conclusions, and they tried yet another test. Glover was in a bad way, but she perked up when her puppets were brought to her. Yet as soon as she held one in her hands, "the children fell into sad fits." Cause and effect: Put a puppet in the hands of a witch and children suffer.

Mather understood that catching Glover presented an exceptional opportunity. Like modern doctors who try to halt the course of a contagious disease by tracing the contact history of a person who is carrying it, ministers would question witches to learn more about the devil and any others he may have converted to his ways. Mather went to visit Glover in jail to question her, and she admitted meeting her prince, the devil, and four others. Mather prayed with her, and he was gratified to report that though she had resisted at first, she wound up thanking him.

Glover was convicted of being a witch and was properly hanged. Witches were never burned in America. Instead of repenting, at the last meeting Glover warned that her death would not help the Goodwin children. According to Mather, as she predicted, "the three children continued in their furnace as before, and it grew rather seven times hotter than it was."

EXPLORING the
invisible world

With his one human suspect gone, Mather now had to use the words of the afflicted

children themselves to lead him
to their remaining tormentors.
For it was the property of these
witches to show something of
themselves as they did their malicious work. Thus eleven-year-old
John Goodwin could see that there
were four evil shapes in the room

with him, and he could almost name them, but not quite.

Again Mather tried a test: If the invisible forms that
only John could see emanated from human beings, hit-

ting one of the specters should
cause an injury to the person.
Rumor had it that an "obnoxious
woman" whose identity Mather hid
suddenly developed a wound just
after the test.

The Goodwin children were in
torment, sometimes barking like
dogs, sometimes purring like cats;
sweating and panting as if they were baking in an oven,
then shivering as if drenched with cold water. Red
streaks showed up on their bodies
where they claimed they were
being beaten with invisible sticks.
One of the boys would be frozen

Published in London in 1681, this series of images
shows spirits gathering, approaching, and then
materializing in a house. The spirits here seem at
first like a swarm of flying devil-dragonflies and
then stiff almost-human ghosts. In New England
most people believed that spirits were all around,
trying to influence humans for good or ill.

and immobile, as if he were nailed to the floor. Then, suddenly, he and the others would seem to fly "with incredible swiftness through the air," with only a toe occasionally touching the floor.

Though the youngest among them was already seven, whenever the children had to dress or undress, they would have tantrums like the wildest toddlers. "It would sometimes cost one of them an hour or two to be undressed in the evening, or dressed in the morning. For if any one went to untie a string, or undo a button about them . . . they would be twisted into such postures as made the thing impossible."

Faced with this extremity of suffering, Mather took young Martha Goodwin into his own home so that he could watch over her and care for her himself. There, daily, he saw her fight invisible presences, go rigid when given food, and struggle to read the Bible even as "her eyes would be strangely twisted and blinded" and her neck seemed on the verge of breaking. Eventually, due to his constant ministrations, she and all the Goodwin children were delivered from the evils that assailed them. Choosing caution over zeal, Mather never revealed the names of any other witches he may have discovered in the process.

Lessons and
WARNINGS   Cotton Mather published his account
of his experiences with the Goodwin children as soon as he could, but not before their father, also named John, added a written postscript. John Goodwin understood

that whatever took place in his family was just. Surely God was afflicting his children because he had failed in "admonishing and instructing" them. Still, that did not make it much easier for him to see his children suffer, "those little bodies, that should be temples for the Holy Ghost to dwell in, should be thus harassed and abused by the devil and his cursed brood." His own helplessness made it worse, for "doctors cannot help, parents weep and lament over them, but cannot ease them." Many people suggested that he try "tricks"—the kind of folk magic often used against witches—but Goodwin resisted. And in the end it was fasting and prayer, and the help of the ministers led by Mather, that delivered his children back to him.

To John Goodwin, all the misery his family experienced was justified. In part, he believed, it happened because he had not been a good enough father. But in a larger sense, he was sure, it was a lesson to all "that prayer is stronger than witchcraft."

For believing Puritans, the episode with the Goodwin children had been harrowing but ultimately a triumph. A witch had been discovered, led to confess, and killed; four children had been afflicted, but all were healed. A great minister had proven to be a caring man who would go to any lengths to help an anguished parent and four children trapped in invisible chains. Incontrovertible proof that evil was real, that the devil was present, and that witches were dangerous had played out in Boston, and yet those same events proved that stalwart ministers and fervent prayer could defeat the worst of the devil's designs. The clear lesson was to watch out for attacks from the invisible world and to rely on the leaders of the community when these attacks came. For any who might be tempted by the Quakers, here was a warning to stick with the true faith.

For skeptics, both of the time and since, a very different set of events had unfolded. A sick old Catholic woman who couldn't even speak English had religious articles in her home. Her garbled "confession" probably was as much a defense of her Catholic faith as anything else—even Mather admitted that Glover sometimes called her spirits her "saints." On this flimsy evidence she was executed. Four children underwent some form of disturbance, which perhaps hints of a rebellion against the very admonitions and instructions their father valued so highly. Perhaps they enjoyed racing about and screaming and getting attention more than being well-behaved "temples for the Holy Ghost." Whatever the initial cause of their ills, soon enough their troubles faded away. Since Mather was both a central actor in the events and the author of the sole account of what took place, it is impossible to know exactly what the children experienced. The lesson of the Goodwin children was that children's games could have serious consequences.

Four years later these two views clashed again in Salem, and those events changed New England in ways neither Mather nor his critics could have imagined.

CHAPTER I

Two salem FAMILIES, 1641–1692

...s for our So[vereign] Lord and Lady the K[ing]...
...That Sarah Buckley Wife of Willia[m]...

In the County of Essex Shoom...
...he Eighteenth day of May ___ ___
...e aforesaid and Divers other dayes an[d]...
...as after Certaine detestable Arts...
...eous Wickedly Malitiously and fel[oniously]...
...ed and Exercised At and in the Tow[ne]...
...nty of Essex ___ ___ Aforesaid in ...
...uttman of Salem ___
...an ___ ___ ___ by whi[ch]...
...hn Puttnam y Day & Yeare afo[resaid]...
...and times both before and after w...
...flicted Consumed Pined wasted c...
...ndry other Acts of Witchcraft b...
...kley ___ Comitted and done before...
...nst our So[vereign] Lord and Lady the...
...rowne & Dignity and the form...

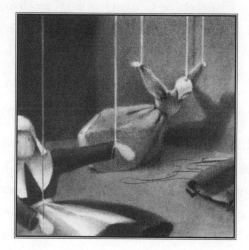

The PUTNAMS
and the PORTERS

Like all children, Ann Putnam Jr. must have grown up listening to her parents, her relatives, and their friends tell stories. The fables, legends, and myths children hear are not only the kind that parents and teachers tell formally—the ones that always end in morals that adults are eager to pass on. There are also the stories adults tell one another, often bitter tales about tricks, conspiracies, and bad people who have managed to bend the rules and come out on top. Those are the stories Ann must have heard again and again, for her powerful family was suffering setbacks, and they were sure they knew why.

Things should have been different. John Putnam came from Berkshire County, near London, to Salem in New England and established a farm there in 1641. The first town established in the Massachusetts Bay Colony, Salem took its name from *shalom,* the Hebrew word for "peace." Its founders wanted Salem to be a place where a settler could prosper while living well with his neighbors, obeying the rules of the Lord. In 1629, three years after the first Europeans arrived in Salem, they defined the shared commitment that was the basis of their community: "We covenant with the Lord and one with another; and do bind ourselves in the presence of God, to walk together in all his ways."

A people bound together to live by God's laws: This pact formed the heart of the Puritan community, and it was built upon a very special kind of test. Puritans did not think a person could do anything to win God's favor. No amount of good works or prayers or donations to the church would help in any way. Salvation was entirely up to God. But when God invited a person to do so, he or she could prepare to receive divine grace. Paradoxically, a key moment came just when the person felt hopeless.

Samuel Sewall was a Boston merchant who was also a devout, sincere Puritan. He would later play an important part in the Salem witch trails. Sewall recorded his spiritual struggles in his diary. At the very moment when he was about to become a full member of his church, he experienced the most extreme doubts. He questioned whether he actually believed in the divinity of Jesus, and he felt he had to admit to the whole congregation "what a great sinner I had been." Similarly, a woman in Wenham, a town near Salem, who was also about to join a church described herself as in "a worse condition than any toad."

Recognizing one's sinfulness and unworthiness was extremely painful and frightening. A woman named Anne Fitch described this vividly: "My sins and God's wrath were so amazing to me that I can't express it, so that though my bodily pain was very great, yet such was the anguish of my spirit that I thought it ten times greater, and so great that no affliction that ever I felt in my life was in any measure like it." Looking clearly at the state of her own soul, the sinner could see how hopeless it was to expect anything from God, how undeserving she was of salvation. But this very agony also opened new space, new room, in a person. If God allowed it, shattered pride permitted the person to experience the sweetness, the beauty, of divine grace.

Once a person was sure that God had given that gift of grace, he could stand before a church and describe how the divine spirit had worked on his soul. If the congregation approved, the saved person could then join them as a full member, a "visible saint." When a male believer stood up and addressed his congregation (women generally spoke privately to elders, then the pastor read the statement out loud), a unique kind of bond was built. In one way, the statement—called a "relation"—was a kind of test. The congregation could decide whether or not that person was only pretending to be saved. In another way, the relation was like the confessions now seen on talk shows and in group therapy sessions. A person admitted his weakness in public, which allowed him to feel fully accepted by the community.

Having a test for membership in a church did more than offer Puritans spiritual comfort. It also brought the hope of overcoming the divisions that keep people apart and of creating a loving community. Within the church, members would "carefully avoid all oppression, griping, and hard dealing, and walk in peace, love, mercy, and equity, towards each other, doing so to others as we would they should do to us." Religion was not an imposed obligation. It was the most precious opportunity to live well with others and in the sight of God.

John Putnam's life in Salem illustrated exactly how well a settler could do in the new land. By the time he died in 1662, he owned nearly eight hundred acres, which gave his three sons a fine inheritance. They, too, prospered, and in 1681 the Putnams were assessed the highest taxes in Salem. This success story did not conflict with the ideal of a shared community. Puritans were expected to work hard and attempt to do well in the world. But the Putnams were farmers, and not all land is good land. This put them on one side of the largest strain on the covenant that bound together the people of Salem: the needs of the farmers against the ambitions of the merchants.

Unfortunately, the family holdings were like so much of New England at the time: too rocky to farm well, too swampy to use as a pasture, with no easy access to rivers, roads, or other convenient routes to markets. The one family effort to find a new way to earn money failed disastrously when an ironworks built to extract ore from their land was burned down by an unhappy employee, leaving the Putnams with nothing but lawsuits. And a new generation of sons was coming of age, which further divided the Putnam lands into eleven plots.

Meanwhile, another family was rising. The Porters came from a background similar to that of the Putnams, but they were finding new routes to prosperity. John Porter arrived in Salem from England at just about the same time as John Putnam, and he also got his family off to a good start. When he died in 1676, he owned more land than anyone else in Salem. More important than the land itself, however, was the location of much of it: on a peninsula knifing into the heart of the Frost Fish River. Salem was the second-largest port in New England, and from their docks and wharves, the Porter family soon became involved in trade. As early as 1658, John traveled to the island of Barbados and served as a witness on a contract for a fellow Salem merchant. The Porter clan was moving away from depending on the unyielding New England

soil and toward links with businessmen in distant
lands.

By 1668 the Salem merchants who watched their
ships sail off to the Caribbean, to France, and to
England had become an elite that was markedly different from the struggling farmers. No longer a village in
which everyone lived on relatively similar farms, the
center of Salem was turning into a town where more
and more people did not own their own land. Instead,
they developed special skills to serve the shipping
industry or to cater to the needs of the merchants.
"Salem Town," as this hub was called, seemed to be a
place for individuals seeking always for their own best
advantage, not a home of the shared values Salem was
meant to embody. Seeing a devotion to commerce as a
threat to religion, ministers began to condemn the
business mentality. The very avenues that offered success to the Porters and their allies were seeming ever
more ominous to the Putnams and the ministers they
supported and trusted. This was one instance of the
most fundamental problem in the whole colony.

All across Massachusetts there were signs that the
Puritan world was fracturing. Originally, the leaders
of the community had set fair prices, so no one could
take advantage of a neighbor's misfortune. They had
made rules that limited the kinds of clothing people
could wear, so everyone had a kind of uniform suited
to his or her standing. They were very strict about who
could join a church, to ensure that each congregation

was a community of true believers who had experienced God's grace. But now the kind of people who were prospering in Salem Town seemed to be living by entirely new standards. They traveled the world in search of profit. They built fine homes and wore lavish clothes. They loosened the rules for church membership. Some even strayed toward Anglicanism or went as far as allowing their children to marry Quakers.

Salem was no longer a home of peace, a community united in faith. Instead, the deep fault line that threatened all of New England—the tensions between merchants and farmers, people looking ahead to their individual futures versus people trying to hold on to a vision of a shared community—shook in every squabble that pitted the Putnams against the Porters.

The
THEFT Faced with powerful opponents they did not like, the Putnams and their allies wanted to split away from Salem Town and form a new township of their own. "Salem Village," as they called it (it is the city of Danvers today), would have its own rules and its own church. The villagers there could preserve the original vision of Puritanism and free themselves from the control and contamination of the high-living Salem Town merchants. But the leaders of Salem Town were not eager to let a substantial part of their town and its tax revenues break away. Over the years the blustery, plain-talking Putnams and the subtle, politically astute

Porters were at odds. In 1672, Salem Village was allowed
to establish a church, but only as a branch of the main
congregation in Salem Town. The conflict about the
villagers' yearning for independence was now played
out in endless quarrels over selecting the pastor for the
new church. And in the midst of these clashes came the
theft.

John Putnam's oldest son was named Thomas.
Thomas was of the generation that did pretty well,
while his own eldest son, Thomas Jr., recognized
that the future was not quite so bright. As the family
venture into ironworking failed and their land-
holdings were sliced into ever-smaller slivers,
Thomas Jr. understood that he needed to make a
fresh start. And he knew just how to do it: by
marrying Ann Carr, a daughter of a wealthy man
in the neighboring town of Salisbury. But when
George Carr died, his male heirs managed to keep
the majority of the property for themselves, leaving
the six daughters and their husbands (including
Thomas Jr.) to divide up the rest in small allot-
ments. The slick Porters and their merchant friends
seemed to control local affairs, and apparently, the
courts were in their service, robbing Thomas of what
he had reason to expect would be his.

This was only the first blow. The courts ruled
against Thomas in 1682. Four years later he got even
worse news. Thomas had six sisters and a brother. But
after his mother died, his fifty-year-old father

remarried one Mary Veren, the widow of a ship captain. Mary was very much a part of the Salem merchant world. Unexpectedly, she bore Thomas Sr. yet
another son, Joseph. When Thomas Sr. died in 1686,
his will brought bitter news: The best part of his
estate, the most fertile lands left from old John's
time, went to Mary and Joseph.

Everyone in the Putnam clan knew whom to blame:
the scheming Mary, their stepmother, and her all-
too-favored son, Joseph. But they could not seem to
convince anyone else of the betrayal that was so obvious to them. The courts upheld Thomas Sr.'s will.
Finally, in 1690, came the last blow. This same Joseph
Putnam, now one of the wealthiest men in Salem, took
a wife. She was Elizabeth Porter, pride of the family
that seemed to rise, as if by magic, even as the hard-
working, salt-of-the-earth Putnams saw what was
rightfully theirs stolen away. To the children of
Thomas Sr.'s first marriage, it must have seemed as if
evil forces, cruel stepmothers, and worse were conspiring to steal their wealth and leave them to flounder
or even perish.

By 1692, then, the stories twelve-year-old Ann
Putnam heard from her mother, Ann, and her father,
Thomas, and all her close relations must have been
very much like the fairy tales we read in books—but with
one deadly difference. For Ann Jr. these stories were
not about long ago and far away. They were the most
basic truths about here and now.

A minister's

WARNINGS Anyone who was called to the ministry of Salem Village was in a very difficult position. The church was created to serve the needs of people such as the Putnams who disliked and distrusted the merchant types of Salem Town. The farmers wanted a minister who would see the world as they did and urge a return to what they saw as an older and truer way of living, leading the way toward a full break with Salem Town. And yet because Salem Village was not yet independent, the wealthy and powerful leaders of Salem Town, such as the Porters, still had great influence on the Salem Village church.

Caught between powerful factions, a string of ministers of the Salem Village church came and went. James Bayley arrived in 1672, married one of Ann Putnam Sr.'s sisters, and yet only managed to hold on to the role until 1680 by defending his position in court. The ongoing strain of his contentious stay may even have led to the early death of his wife. George Burroughs lasted just three years before returning to the community in what is now Maine from which he had been recruited. Though he could not know it at the time, his entanglement with the festering antagonisms of Salem Village had only begun. Following Burroughs, Deodat Lawson stuck it out for five years, during which time tempers in Salem heated. With the Putnams taking the lead, the Salem Village faction was determined to have its church stand on its own, with

no links to that of Salem Town. But the townsfolk held
off the villagers, and Lawson, the Putnams' man, left.
Only when the new minister arrived,
in 1688, did Salem Town
finally allow Salem Village to
run its own church.

The Putnams and
their allies were sure
that Samuel Parris, the
new minister they
selected, would be just
the man to uphold
their values and com-
plete their break from
Salem Town. Indeed,
Parris was and he did—but
for the wrong reasons. He
became a minister only after
he failed at being just the kind
of merchant who was prospering in Salem Town. If he

This image on a gold locket is believed to
represent the Reverend Samuel Parris,
and it is the only likeness of him that has
survived.

favored the older ways of the farmers in the hinter-
lands of Salem Village, that was probably because he
himself had been unable to master the complications
of trade and commerce. He, too, had a bitter edge of
envy for those who found easy prosperity in sending
ships and cargoes to ports all around the world.

As Parris established himself in his church, his sermons turned again and again to one theme: the clash

between good people banding together in a Christian community and liars who pretended to be good but schemed and plotted for their own ends. The danger of deception and falsehood was everywhere, even in one's own family, because devils, witches, and evil forces were ready to seize on wicked people and put their greed to satanic purposes.

By February 1692, Parris was speaking of an impending war between good and evil, in which everyone had to be on the alert and ready for battle. Since the early days of the Puritans the front line had shifted. There were still wolves and Indians nearby, but the more dangerous enemy was within the community itself—or even closer than that.

Perhaps Parris was speaking about things he had seen with his own eyes. For the hellish conflict was already starting, in his own home.

Two Mysteries

s for our Sov[er]ei[g]n Lord and Lady the K[ing]

That Sarah Buckly Wife of William[?]

In the County of Essex Shoomn[?]

the Eighteenth day of May — —

aforesaid and divers other days an[d]

as after Certaine detestable Arts

called Witchcrafts Maliciously and fell[oniously]

and Exercised At and in the Tow[n]

ty of Essex — Aforesaid in s[aid]

man of Salem — —

— — by which[?]

[Jo]hn Puttnam y[e] Day & Yeare Afor[esaid]

and times both before and after w[?]

wicked Consumed Pined Wasted & [?]

ndry other Acts of Witchcraft by [?]

kly — Comittand done before [?]

st our Sov[er]ei[g]n Lord and Lady the [?]

rowne & Dignity and the forme[r]

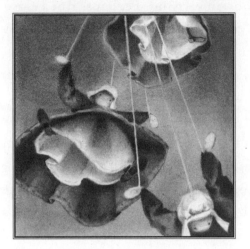

The first
MYSTERY   No one knows for sure how it began.
From the time of the very start of the outbreak of
witchcraft accusations, we have just fragments of evidence—like the pot shards and chipped stones of
ancient civilizations found at an archaeological site.
These frustrating hints and clues often seem to just
about add up to a satisfying story, and for generations
authors blurred the details and made the events seem
simpler and clearer than the evidence actually shows.
Perhaps Samuel Parris's nine-year-old daughter,
Elizabeth, called Betty, and his eleven- or twelve-year-
old (we are not sure about her age) niece, Abigail

Williams, were using some old English folk magic, and it went horribly wrong. Perhaps. But a close reading of the one record that suggests this origin leaves as many questions as it offers answers.

John Hale, a minister who was experienced in dealing with cases of witchcraft and was personally involved with the events in Salem, left us one puzzling clue that has been twisted into a vivid narrative over the centuries. Troubled by what he saw as a good cause gone wrong, he wrote an essay five years after the trials that both affirmed the reality of witchcraft and admitted that "a great deal of innocent blood" had been shed "in the Christian world, by proceeding upon unsafe principles, in condemning persons for . . . witchcraft." It was simultaneously an apology for errors in Salem and a defense of the need to be vigilant against witches. That confusion of motives makes it hard to know how to evaluate his words.

Hale's essay first recounts the story of Salem, beginning "in the latter end of the year 1691," meaning sometime in January or February of what we think of as 1692. Much later on, in a chapter on the ways in which people in many different places unknowingly fall into witchcraft by using charms, incantations, and spells, he says, "I fear some young persons, through a vain curiosity to know their future condition, have tampered with the Devil's tools so far that hereby one door was opened to Satan to play those pranks, anno [year] 1692." Perhaps this refers to the events that ini-

tiated the crisis in Salem, which did mainly take place
in 1692, even by his calendar.

Or perhaps not. For Hale goes on to tell a grue-
some story that no other commentator recorded and
no other scholar has been able to confirm. He says that
"one of the afflicted persons who (as I was credibly
informed) did try with an egg and a glass to find her
future husband's calling, till there came up a coffin,
that is, a specter in likeness of a coffin. And she was
afterwards followed with a diabolical molestation to
her death, and so died a single person—a just warning
to others to take heed of handling the Devil's weapons
lest they get a wound thereby."

Hale claims that through prayer and confession he
was able to heal the other "young person."

Two girls dabbling in foretelling their futures by
dropping an egg white into water and interpreting the
shapes that formed, then being terrified by what they
saw. . . . Could they be Betty and Abigail? We know that
an afflicted Betty was sent away to stay with a family
friend, and she did slowly recover, though there is no
evidence that Hale visited and ministered to her. And,
after being quite active in the trials, Abigail disappears
from the records. It is tempting to suppose that Hale
was writing about her and that she died tormented by
her visions. But despite the careful research of many
scholars, there is absolutely no record of Abigail's fate.
And there is good reason to doubt Hale completely,
for no other source mentions his story—an account

that would have been perfect evidence for those who wanted to defend the trials. After all, it is the only instance in which one of the people who were afflicted in 1692 died from her devilish wounds. All the other people who came to court complaining of being assaulted and abused by witches easily recovered, no matter how grievous their suffering. If Hale was writing about Abigail, a leading accuser in the trials, why didn't anyone else point to her terrible death as proof of the power of the devil?

Hale might have been referring to a different case, not the girls in early 1692 (1691 by his calendar), but others in late 1692. In October of that year court records show that Sarah Cole from the neighboring town of Lynn and "others" used a "Venus glass and an egg" to find out "what trade their sweethearts should be." Maybe Hale was mixing up a variety of cases to emphasize his "just warning": Look what can happen if you dabble with the devil; you might even lose your life. As happens so often in studying Salem, we have almost enough evidence to tell a true story full of juicy details, but not quite.

Whatever the cause, Betty and Abigail soon began behaving very strangely. According to a sympathetic Hale, they seemed to be "pinched and bitten by invisible agents; their arms, necks, and backs turned this way and that, and returned back again. . . . Sometimes they were taken dumb, their mouths stopped, their throats choked, their limbs wracked and tormented."

Yet from the first, others saw it differently. A more suspicious author named Robert Calef, who opposed all of the accusations and convictions that followed, described the same girls this way: They "began to act, after a strange and unusual manner, viz., as by getting into holes, and creeping under chairs and stools, and to use sundry odd postures and antic gestures, uttering foolish, ridiculous speeches, which neither they themselves nor any other could make sense of."

Both skeptics and those convinced by the girls' agonies shared one perception: The Salem girls were experiencing something very similar to the afflictions of the Goodwin children about whom Cotton Mather had written. There is every chance that young people in Salem would have read or heard about his book. From the first, the Salem story was a crossing point of different beliefs. The girls may have been practicing the "little sorceries" Mather had warned about. Soon they enacted the behavior he described. Did this mean that he was right and that evil was nearby? Or did it imply that the girls were good readers and good mimics?

Whatever was bothering the girls, it was quite contagious. Very quickly, others in the community showed signs of serious disturbance: bites, fits, tortured bodies, if you believed the reports; silly dramatics, if you did not. The infection seemed to travel along the lines of the poisonous rifts in Salem. No one in Salem Town was affected. But in Salem Village the Putnam family, the leaders of the farm group, and those most active in supporting Parris were the hardest hit by the trouble. Or you might also say they became the center of the action. Twelve-year-old Ann Putnam Jr., her mother, Ann Sr., a seventeen-year-old servant living with the Putnams named Mercy Lewis, and another seventeen-year-old relative and neighbor named Mary Walcott all showed signs of affliction. Elizabeth Hubbard, the seventeen-year-old niece of a local physician, and Mary Warren, a twenty-year-old servant, did too. Something was very visibly wrong in Salem.

The first mystery is why strange signs of affliction began in the first place—how to interpret Hale's sympathetic but enigmatic account and evaluate it against Calef's complete skepticism. However you resolve that will lead you to the even more puzzling second mystery.

The second
MYSTERY If Hale was talking about Betty Parris and Abigail Williams, then it would be easy to picture a scenario such as this: Nine-year-old Betty, the daughter of a minister, knew she was doing something forbidden when she tried to see the future; and when she got scared by something she saw, she felt doubly ashamed at what she had done. Perhaps, like Elizabeth Knapp after her chores were mysteriously finished for her, Betty began to feel evil. Then, haunted by her sense of shame and guilt, Betty may have acted in the ways she associated with people possessed by the devil.

The natural next step after that would have been for Betty to seek help in expunging the vile forces from her. Her elders, just like Hale in his essay, would chastise her for her experiments, but she would be forgiven.

But why would this behavior spread? It could be that many of the younger women in the area, from children to the recently married, were using folk rituals such as the Venus glass. For some, the practices would have been quite unremarkable, simply the passing on of traditions they had learned from their mothers, relatives, and friends. Others might have been searching for new answers outside of the stern words of their ministers and the demands of their austere faith. According to the nineteenth-century Salem minister and local historian Charles Upham, for example, Ann Putnam Sr. had never completely recovered from the death of her sister (the wife of the Reverend Bayley) and the loss of one of her own children. She could have been drawn to experimentation with contacting the spirits of the dead.

As Betty roiled in her own sense of shame and fear, her peers might have felt a need to show and thus exorcise their sense of being tainted. If one dabbler in the occult began to behave strangely, anyone who had done some secret experimenting herself might grow very anxious about any twitch or jerk that suggested she was actually possessed. Some might even rush to their ministers with exaggerated symptoms, just to get checked out and cleared.

A set of individuals who were privately using practices their community officially condemned suddenly
acts out in bizarre ways. This can be seen as a form of
confession as well as a plea to be exorcised and healed.
This story makes sense, at least as a theory. But then
the Parris episode took a strange turn, for the focus
shifted completely away from the girls' or young
women's responsibility for allowing the devil to enter

their lives. Abruptly and inexplicably, they became victims. The issue changed from "How did I let Satan
in?" to "Who is using Satan against me?" The turning
point came with a slave woman named Tituba.

Discovered by the historian Elaine Breslaw, these two images *(above and
left)* are of a 1676 inventory of slaves from the Barbados plantation of
Samuel Thompson. "Tattuba" appears on both lists, three quarters of
the way down in the right-hand column, and is underlined. This may
mean that Tituba grew up on this plantation.

For all of the Reverend Parris's thunder about the treacherous world just outside his small congregation, he could not entirely shut out the contacts that trade brought to Salem. Parris, who grew up in Barbados, owned Tituba, an Indian slave who was probably from the Caribbean, and her husband, aptly named John Indian. The presence of this Caribbean couple in New England was just as much a product of the links binding Massachusetts, the West Indies, and England as had been John Porter's visit to Barbados. As much as devout Protestants in New England saw themselves as living their own lives by their own rules, and as much as the farmers of Salem Village sought to break off from the more worldly merchants of Salem Town, everyone in the English-speaking world was slowly being drawn together in bonds of commerce and law, writing and conversation.

Tituba seems to have been an intelligent, adaptable woman who quickly learned from her owners. Apparently, a neighbor named Mary Sibley asked—or insisted—that John, and perhaps Tituba, help her to use a magical method to find out if Betty and Abigail were being afflicted by a witch. If the girls' urine was baked with rye flour into a kind of biscuit and fed to a dog, the animal was supposed to lead to the witch or even speak her name. Or the witch herself would be drawn to the animal. This ritual was yet another that the Puritans had brought with them from England.

The Tituba who appears in many novels, plays, and

even older history books about Salem brings pagan, voodoolike island beliefs and rituals with her to New England. It is not surprising, then, that she was at the heart of the case from the start. According to these often lurid accounts, she is responsible for teaching young New England girls new forms of trafficking with spirits. But the slave woman who appears in the actual records is insistent that she used only the magic taught to her by her English neighbors and mistresses. There is absolutely no reason to doubt her. And if the Hale story of the egg and glass is about Betty and her cousin, then Tituba was not involved at all in the beginning.

The second
MYSTERY deepens

On February 25, 1692, Mary Sibley involved John and maybe Tituba (two different records contradict themselves on this point) in the rye cake test. Shortly thereafter the first witch was revealed. She was Tituba herself. The two girls cried out that the Indian woman "did pinch, prick, and grievously torment them, and that they saw her here and there, where no body else could. Yea they could tell where she was, and what she did, when out of their human sight." Tituba was not only herself, but an evil ghost of herself that haunted and tormented the girls.

The whole story of the test is confusing, especially from the point of view of the beliefs of the time. If Tituba was involved in baking the cake, no one raised the most obvious question: Why would a real witch conversant with magic spells accurately perform a test solely designed to catch herself? Hale later reported that Tituba had been trained in detecting witches by her English mistress in Barbados, who truly was a witch. If Tituba believed the test would work, wouldn't she have been able to subvert it?

In reality, the test had little to do with anything Tituba did. It simply gave the girls a way to speak without being responsible for their words. The girls may have associated Tituba with an occult force that they wanted to tap but that they also feared was taking them over. Tituba was both the conduit to the beyond and the embodiment of its threat. The test gave them a way to voice these feelings.

We do not know what Tituba looked like or even what kind of "Indian" she was. There were no native Indians still living on Barbados in her time, but both conquered Wampanoags from New England and Arawaks from the area that is now Guyana and Venezuela were brought to the island as slaves. Yet the specifics of Tituba's appearance and heritage probably were not what influenced the girls. The fact that she was an Indian was enough.

The vexing Sir Edmond Andros was removed as governor of New England in 1689 even as William and Mary, a new king and queen, were installed in England. What would these changes mean for New England and its Puritan ways? Increase Mather sailed off to plead the case for his people, arguing that they should be allowed to retain their own particular form of church government and political organization. No one knew how that would turn out. Without secure protection from England, New England's borders felt all the less safe. And the French and Indians were rumored to be planning new attacks, renewing the warfare that had ended in 1676. Rumor had it that French Catholic priests—rather like modern clerics who support terror—inspired their Indian allies by telling them it was a good deed to murder the English, who were responsible for killing Jesus. Though it was the Indians who had suffered most from the recent war, by the 1690s the New Englanders were feeling the threat of the Indians with ever-growing force.

One of the women later accused of being a witch spoke of her terror of Indians and her dreams of fighting them. The devil she described both used this fear and embodied it. He "appeared to her in the shape of a tawny man and promised to keep her from the Indians." The devil was an Indian, yet a tempting guardian who would keep the Indians away. Surely for some New Englanders, Indians were figures of nightmare: all the terrors and dangers of the New World manifested in human form.

For Cotton Mather, the danger of Indians took a different form. Looking at Indian religious practices through his eyes is like having a vision of hell. He imagined that in their "wigwams" Indian sorcerers were raising the spirits of devils "in the shapes of bears and snakes and fires." Indians stood for the pagan world of magic he tried to stamp out and the evil forces he had to combat.

The historian Mary Beth Norton has recently identified and vividly described a series of conflicts in just this period in which Wabanaki people aided by French Catholics devastated what was then the northern portion of the colony and is now Maine. Through wonderful detective work she has shown that ten of the people who accused others of being witches—including Mary Walcott and, most significantly, Mercy Lewis— experienced traumas in these conflicts, such as the murder of close relatives or the loss of property and standing. In addition, she has linked twenty-three of the accused to the events in Maine, as well as thirteen of the most important judges, jurors, clergymen, and officials in the trials. In the minds of the accusers, accused, and judges, the external attacks that were imperiling New England settlements and ravaging families were immediately and definitively linked to manifestations of devilish activity in and around Salem.

Once the young women of Salem began to feel unsafe due to their dabbling in the occult, they might well have thought of Tituba—the Indian in their midst—as their fears made flesh. But here again the story takes another twist. It is not hard to picture Tituba serving as the scapegoat for the troubles of the first two girls and for the spreading symptoms.

Something very like that may have started to take place. But Salem was too volatile a place for its tensions to be healed with the sacrifice of just one.

There are two different versions of Samuel Parris's reaction to yet one more use of magic in his own home. According to one account, even after the rye cake test, he was a model of caution and patience. He asked a number of local doctors to examine the afflicted girls. The doctors' judgment was sobering: This was a case involving evil spirits, not physical ills. Parris's next remedy was much like that of Cotton Mather in the Goodwin case: a combination of prayer and fasting. When that tactic did not seem to work, he called on sober and established men, perhaps John Hale included, to give him counsel. Thus Parris's behavior was the exact opposite of the harsh, frenzied, and blameful pattern often associated with Puritan ministers.

This first account claims that Parris did condemn the use of the rye cake test but not Tituba or John for conducting it. Instead, he criticized Mary Sibley, the neighbor who oversaw the ritual. But according to a second version of these same events, Parris seemed very affected by the test, so much so that Robert Calef reported a very disturbing story about his reaction. He wrote that Tituba later claimed Parris had beaten and abused her until she confessed to being a witch and named others. Parris might have beaten his slave if he wanted her to confess and take the blame for everything. But his demand that she name others makes sense only if Parris believed the diabolical test had yielded true results.

This question of how to evaluate information that came from magical, perhaps devilish, sources was the central issue that came up from the beginning of the Salem case—and the one that made Salem different from other historical cases of witchcraft. The devil was known as the "father of lies." How could one trust a test that called on his powers? Speaking to his congregation, Parris himself said that the test was "going to the Devil for help against the Devil." If the test was not reliable, why would Parris believe it, beat his slave, and insist that she name other witches? Either there was some other cause for his suspicion that has been lost to history or the popular traditions of folk rituals and magical beliefs were convincing even to trained ministers, and all their care to spurn both "white" and "black" practices was fading away.

In the early months of 1692 many in Salem were so on edge that what people saw as accusations of witchcraft, manifestations of witchcraft, and devilish misinformation about witchcraft all blended together and confirmed one another's reality. Everywhere you turned, there was more evidence that the devil was nearby, even in the spread of lies and half-truths. Everything seemed covered in a miasma of deceit—the devil's trail—and there was no apparent way out but to find the witches, the devil's agents, execute them, and return the community to safety in the sight of God.

Something about this case was so strange, so disturbing, that even ministers lost their way. The eerie powers of the invisible realm seemed to be manifesting themselves everywhere, too real to ignore.

Given the choice between seeing the suffering of their neighbors as God's punishment for dabbling in the occult or as symptoms of devilish, Indian-like, witch-driven attacks, more and more people in Salem chose anger over penitence. Instead of faith turning them inward to conscience, it pushed them outward to attack. For reasons we only imperfectly understand, a culture of blame had taken root, and it would require an agonizing year of accusations, trials, and deaths before the balance shifted back to introspection.

And yet the devil was not the only one capable of lying. Tituba, who was angry at Parris when she made the accusation, could have made up the story of the beating. Nor is it certain that Calef, the critic of the ministers, wrote it down accurately and did not invent the incident himself. One more compelling clue that seems to hint at the deep currents of the story itself turns out to be a fragment whose meaning can only be guessed at and debated.

CHAPTER III

The Mysteries End and the Hearings Begin

... for our Sou[r] Lord and Lady the K[ing]
That Sarah Buckley Wife of Willia[m]

In the County of Essex Shoom[aker?]
the Eighteenth day of May

aforesaid and divers other days an[d]
... as after Certaine detestable Arts
... Wickedly Maliciously and fol[oniously]
... and Exercised at and in the Tou[n]
...ty of Essex aforesaid in ...
... ttman of Salem

... by whi[ch]
...hn Puttnam y Day & Yeare afo[resaid]
...and times both before and after ...
flicted Consumed Pined Wasted C...
...undry other Acts of Witchcraft b...
...kley Committ and done before ...
...st our Sou[r] Lord and Lady the
...rowne & Dignity and the form...

The usual
SUSPECTS Whatever forces drove the girls to cry
out against Tituba could not be soothed with merely
one accusation. The girls quickly named two other
sources for their suffering: Sarah Good and Sarah
Osborne. All three suspects could have been selected as
a kind of computer-model average of all the previous
New England witchcraft accusations on record. Good
was in her late thirties, poor, and not close to others;
even her own husband thought she might be a witch.
Forced to beg, she often seemed to grumble and mut-
ter when people spurned or ignored her. She was a living embodiment of the scorned woman in the story of

Sleeping Beauty. As for Osborne, she had gotten into trouble for living with a man after her husband died and for skipping church services for over a year. And Tituba was an Indian slave. An Indian, a difficult woman, and a woman people talked and complained about—the girls named just the right suspects.

Fighting demons with spiritual weapons such as prayer was up to individuals and their ministers. But at this point the rules shifted. On February 29, leap day, Ann Putnam Jr.'s father, Thomas, and three others asked the law to step in. They wanted the three women brought to court for a pretrial hearing. Though this session could not lead to a sentence, it could uncover enough evidence to put witches in jail until a full-fledged trial began. Two local dignitaries, Jonathan Corwin and John Hathorne (Nathaniel Hawthorne's direct ancestor) now served as judges. They were later joined by another prominent townsman, Bartholomew Gedney. The judges sent men out to bring in the three suspects. They were to meet their accusers—Betty Parris, Abigail Williams, Ann Putnam Jr., and Elizabeth Hubbard—the next day at an inn. Anyone in the town who wanted to attend the hearing was permitted to come.

All the court had to do was to indict three witches, and a strange and unpleasant episode could have ended, perhaps with a dismissal, as was usual, or even with a few unremarkable convictions. But when the accused faced the judges, it quickly became clear that the crisis in Salem had just begun.

By now all of Salem must have known about the weird, eerie behavior of the girls and young women around the Reverend Parris's home, the accusations of witchcraft, and the moment of reckoning that was about to come. Young and old flocked to the inn to see for themselves if and how the demons were to be exposed. According to Charles Upham, there were too many people to fit the space, and the hearing was therefore moved to the town's meetinghouse.

Sarah Good denied doing any evil, which sent the girls into a frenzy of "torture and torment." Face-to-face, at close quarters, it must have been quite a scene: the stern judges seated at a long table in front of the pulpit, looking at the crowd; the young women, seemingly unable to control their own bodies or to find any peace; the accused witches—unpopular to begin with—seeing the faces of their neighbors judging them and trying to respond to the judges' probing questions. Asked to explain why the victims were suffering so much, Good finally agreed that Osborne was a witch. Hearing this, the accusers suddenly recovered for the moment. But Good had too many enemies, even in her own family, to be spared on the basis of simply blaming someone else.

The accusers responded to Osborne exactly as they had to Good: by being "hurt, afflicted, and tortured" in her presence. And that was only a small part of it. They claimed her specter, her ghostly self, had been assaulting them even when she was far away. Osborne

was equally fervent in denying she was a witch. In her
defense she raised a point that was ignored at first but
could never entirely be dismissed. In the end, it was
one of the reasons serious people began to question
the trials. If the devil used her "likeness" to do harm,
she argued, that was not her fault. She was bringing
up the ambiguity that plagued the case from the start:
If the girls let in the devil, if the rye cake test was diabolical, if evil ghosts in the shapes of townspeople
were afflicting people, why couldn't the devil alone be
responsible? Why assume witches in the town were
assisting him? How could you trust any evidence
tainted by the devil's hand?

Judge Hathorne did not find this possibility significant. And considering the scene, it might have
been hard to weigh out a subtle theological issue. He
was faced with a battery of girls and women, howling,
suffering, seemingly under the worst form of invisible
assault right before his eyes. These victims were from
some of the most important families in Salem Village.
The rest of the room was filled with anxious, eager
townspeople sensing that the very worst of evils was
about to be revealed. Perhaps right here, in his court,
the source of all of the colony's recent afflictions—the
troubles in England, the ominous Indians, the weird
Quakers, the decline in faith—would be exposed. And
standing against that almost electric charge in the air
stood only an outcast woman speaking for herself.

Hathorne pressed on, questioning Osborne, and

found that she, too, was haunted by fears of Indians. As the clerk recorded her testimony, "she was frightened one time in her sleep and either saw or dreamed that she saw a thing like an Indian all black which did pinch her in her neck and pulled her by the back part of her head to the door of the house." This devil later whispered in her ear, telling her not to go to church, but she resisted. The judge was not convinced. After all, she was notorious for not coming to meetings. Osborne claimed she had been ill, but it seemed her own words condemned her.

Two women faced their accusers and the court, fought back against the charges, and were unable to defend themselves. But Tituba, the first person accused—and as an Indian slave, perhaps the most likely person to be blamed—did something completely different. At first she, too, denied pinching or in any way harming the children; at one point, in fact, she said she loved Betty and would not hurt her. Then something happened. Perhaps her training as a slave, ever alert to picking up cues from her master, took over.

Tituba confessed. She took the judges, the court, the afflicted girls, and the people of Salem crowded into the darkened meetinghouse on a journey. And frightening as her story was, it was also calming. Now, finally, everyone had a clear truth that they could believe. Tituba's confession was a map of a dreamland of evil. And for the next few months people treated this dream world as more true than anything they could see with their daylight eyes.

TITUBA'S

confession It must have been obvious to Tituba that standing up against the judges would never work. Instead, she figured out a way to agree with their accusations while always excusing herself. Even as she was admitting evil with her words, in her behavior she was a model of cooperation and contrition. Tituba changed before the court's eyes. She was not an angry, scheming, loudmouthed witch; she was sweet, cooperative, and eager to help. She even began to suffer from the same afflictions as her accusers, as if an angry devil were torturing her and trying to silence her before she revealed his plot. Tituba's performance in court made her story believable, and it saved her life.

Reading Tituba's words in the trial records is like watching a fascinating theatrical performance. When challenged about who was hurting the children, she ventured one surly statement—"The devil for ought I know"—before quickly changing her tone. The devil had, in fact, asked her to serve him, she admitted. He came with four other women, including Good and Osborne. She had seen the four with a mysterious "tall man" in Boston just the previous night, and they had bullied her into harming the girls. Did she give in? "Yes, but I will hurt them no more." And then she said she was sorry she had done any harm.

The room must have suddenly quieted, for as Tituba began to confess, the girls' horrible pains stopped. The judges could immediately see that they would not have to fight with her to get her to confess, so they began to try to use her—as Mather had in Boston with the Goodwin children—to learn more about the devil. We do not know why in this case, unlike so many others, the judges tended to believe that the accused were witches. But it is clear that once Tituba began to confess, they were reassured by her words.

As the questioning moved away from her guilt to her experiences as a victim of the forces of evil, Tituba had ever more elaborate and amazing things to report. The devil came to her in the form of a hog and also a giant black dog. In his human guise the devil had a yellow bird that was a kind of pet. Witches were known to have such "familiars," which took animal form and were fed by a weird extra breast their masters or mistresses grew. And as with Elizabeth Knapp, the devil made the most enticing promises to Tituba. "He had more pretty things," she told the court, "that he would give me if I would serve him."

Tituba may have invented these details on the spur of the moment. But there is also a hint in a second version of the court transcript that suggests she was speaking about actual experiences. There, she explains that the man who appeared to her and intimidated her into harming the girls came "just as I was going to sleep." When she was asked for more details about the witches' meeting in Boston, Tituba gave an answer that almost sounds like modern Halloween stories, but with a key difference: She traveled invisibly, as a spirit. How did she get there? "We ride upon sticks and are there presently." Did that mean they went through the trees or over them? "We see no thing but are there." The next day she went a step further. Asked how often she went to Boston, she replied, "I was never at Boston." In other words, she was not physically there; her spirit had flown to the gathering. That's why it could get there instantly.

For Tituba, dreams and actual events were blurring together. More generally, in New England society at the time there was not a clear line of distinction between the two. Many argued that dreams contained prophecies, revelations, truths more real than daily life, and there was no other clear and common explanation of what else they were. It is possible that Tituba dreamed of meeting a sinister tall man and four evil women who offered her fine things and later demanded that she serve them. One of the evil women, she reported, wore clothes similar to those she had seen when she lived with the Parris family in Boston: "a black silk hood with a white silk hood under it." Tituba's adult life had been in service to well-dressed people who insisted she obey them. Her confession may have been the reverse of the dreams Puritans had of scary Indians: an Indian dream of scary Puritans. Whatever the source, the court heard her visions, fantasies, or dreams as facts.

Whether it was a folk-magic test to expose a witch, young women having fits that they claimed were caused by specters, or Tituba describing the flights of her spirit, the question of how to evaluate the interaction of the invisible world of ghosts and dreams with the common world was the central problem of the trials.

As her confession went on, Tituba became less and less hesitant, and her accounts turned more and more elaborate. Sarah Good, she revealed, had a yellow bird familiar that she fed by letting it suck between her fingers. Sarah Osborne's familiars were even stranger. One was "a thing with a head like a woman with two legs and wings." Another was a hairy creature that walked on two legs like a man. This latter monster had appeared just the night before in front of the fire in the Reverend Parris's home. In describing this creature, perhaps Tituba was

A witch and the forms taken by her familiars, from a 1621 book. Though the black cat is the animal most frequently associated with witches in children's books, the birds shown here are what Tituba and many of the other accusers kept seeing in Salem.

calling on traditional tales from her own childhood in South America, which told of evil *kenaima*s—little people who lived in the forest and came out at night to do harm.

While she told of creatures that had not previously been part of New England lore, Tituba also spoke of the key event she must have known the judges wanted to hear. When she was questioned for a second day, she said the devil claimed he was a god, demanded she serve him for six years, and brought a book with him. The judges were paying close attention. When asked what the book looked like and whether he asked her to put her name in it, Tituba hesitated. "No, not yet, for mistress called me into the other room." But then it seems she caught on to what the judges wanted. "He said write and set my name to it." And she did. She made her mark in blood in the devil's book. The judges had now heard from Tituba exactly what the law called for: a confession of the devil's pact. They pressed on. "Did you see any other marks in the book?" Then came the answer that ensured the trials would go on and on and on: "Yes, a great many."

Tituba had seen with her own eyes exactly what the girls' fits seemed to suggest—namely, that many people had signed themselves over to the devil. The judges seized the opportunity to discover more about the sources of evil in their community. They knew Tituba could not read, but perhaps the devil had left some clues. "Did he tell you the names of them?" Typically, Tituba gave an answer that pleased the judges but said little. The names she heard, she said, were those of

Good and Osborne—the two women already known by the court. How many names were there? If the judges could not get the names of all the witches, at least they would know how many they needed to find. "Nine," she answered, six or seven more than the judges knew about (depending on whether she counted her own mark). And where did these witches live? "Some in Boston and some here in this town, but he would not tell me where they were."

Tituba gave an amazing performance that ended the stumbling, confusing first phase of the outbreak. The judges, the people of Salem, and the great ministers of New England heard in detail what they had previously only suspected. Their worst fears were confirmed. A great conspiracy of evil forces was at work under the devil's direction. Tituba was sent to prison, but then she was almost forgotten. She no longer mattered, and she survived the trials. It was her words that counted. They told everyone what to look for: witches and their spooky familiars; spirits that could fly and appear in other places; the devil seeking names for his dark book; and a mysterious tall man dressed in black who seemed to be the satanic ringleader. These were the themes that would come up again and again for the rest of the year.

Tituba's words changed everything: no more confusion about inviting the devil or being attacked by witches, no more need for questionable magical tests or sober doctors' examinations. There was no longer any question of why people in Salem were being afflicted with disturbing symptoms: Witches were taking their dark toll. The only issues were how many evildoers there were, who was their leader, and how this horrid infection could be stamped out. Now each defendant would not only have to protest his or her own innocence but bring into question a larger story that more and more people were sure was true. This meant the trials were simultaneously about individuals and about the basic belief in witchcraft that most people shared.

CHAPTER IV

The Accuser: Ann Putnam Jr.

s for our Sou[r] Lord and Lady the Kin[g]

That Sarah Buckley Wife of Willia[m]

In the County of Essex Shoom[aker]

[t]he Eighteenth day of May

aforesaid and divers other days an[d]

as after Certaine detestable Arts

[call]ed Witchery Malitiously and foll[oniously]

[use]d and Exercised At and in the Tow[ne]

[Coun]ty of Essex Aforesaid in u[pon]

[the body] of Salem

[An]n Puttnam y[e] Day &[c] Years Afor[esaid]

[and at sundr]y times both before and after w[as]

[afl]icted Consumed Pined Wasted &[c]

[by su]ndry other Acts of Witchcraft by

[the sd Buck]ley Comitted done before [&c]

[again]st Our Sou[r] Lord and Lady the

[C]rowne & Dignity and the forme[r]

Biting, pinching, and CHOKING

Ann Putnam Jr. was there, at the center of everything. Whenever judges needed a confirmation that a witch was harming someone, Ann gave it. Whenever a new set of cases started, spreading the circle of the accused, Ann spoke up. Whenever a witness wavered, starting to take back her confessions or accusations, Ann was sure to find evidence that she, too, was a witch, cowing the wavering witness into silence. Of the nineteen people whom the law was responsible for hanging, Ann Putnam Jr. is known to have testified against seventeen. She was the voice, and the suffering body, of the accusing victims.

If we believe what she told the court, her daily life must have been a torment. Ghosts appeared to her at night, telling her who had murdered them and leaving her to challenge her monstrous neighbors in court. And in daylight, often when she was left alone, and again every time she came face-to-face with the ever-growing circle of exposed witches, she was tortured. She, her mother, her neighbors, and her relations reacted so intensely, and in such similar ways, to the alleged witches that the judges, the crowd, and many visitors were certain the defendants were guilty, no matter what they said in court.

March 3, for example, must have been terrifying. The apparition or evil spirit of Sarah Good's young daughter Dorothy (Dorcas) fastened on to Ann's throat and "almost" choked her. When her intent wasn't murderous, the spirit pinched and bit Ann, trying to force her to sign the spirit's evil book and become a witch herself. That same day another specter, the apparition of Elizabeth Proctor, attacked Ann in exactly the same way, nearly choking her and biting and pinching her. That ghost would later return and urge Ann "vehemently" to "write in her book." Ann reported events such as these day after day after day.

Who *was* Ann Putnam Jr.? At twelve years old she was suddenly the center of attention in Salem, speaking out in the form of visions, dreams, physical assaults—her own version, perhaps, of the stories of dark treachery she had heard from her parents.

Sometimes joined by her mother, who was troubled by both personal tragedy and the Putnams' history of misfortune, sometimes leading her, Ann Jr. was now the voice of the family. She could have been a kind of reverse Carrie—of the Stephen King novel and the movie of the same name—using accusations of occult powers to destroy everyone she felt had hurt her and her family. Did she enjoy her sense of power? Did she actively conspire with her relatives and friends to plan their performances? Or were she and the others merely masterful at watching one another, picking up cues and sensing what each would cry out next, to build a picture of misery that seemed too real and too unified to be invented? On this point one set of experts is at odds with another.

It is possible that Ann went past settling scores and even delighted in destroying other people in town, bringing them down, adults and children, outcasts and leaders, humbling them, forcing them to squirm before the judges, knowing that they would die. Once she got a taste of this brew of vengeance, malice, cruelty, and exquisite power, perhaps it became addictive. And once she began to send her neighbors to their deaths, how could she ever turn back? She might have kept describing evil ghosts trying to force her to sign their book because she felt she had entered into a game that became a plot, an obsession rippling through her circle of friends, her family, her neighbors, her town, and finally all of New England; a game that she could now never stop. In portraying the pact she was desperate to resist, she might actually have been telling people what it felt like to be part of the mad craze that had become her life. We know just enough to invent images of Ann that seem to fit her behavior. But because we cannot answer the most basic questions about her behavior—What were her motivations? What did she think she was doing? Was she driven by subconscious drives, or was she involved in a fully thought-out plot?—we do not know enough to understand her. And Ann is just part of the story.

If it took Ann to drive on the accusations that captivated Salem, it also took a Salem community already filled with rumors, fears, and nightmares turned into daily visions to give Ann a stage. It is as if fairy tales were stepping out of the pages of books and taking over the town. For instance, on the evening of the very first hearing in which Tituba confessed, two men walking in town heard a sound that alarmed them. It was no usual night sound, and they heard it over and over again. Frightened, they searched for the source of the eerie noise and found "a strange and unusual beast lying on the ground." When they approached it, the creature "vanished away." Suddenly, it was not an odd shape, but rather the shades of two or three women whom they "took to be Sarah Good, Sarah Osborne, and Tituba."

Nights in Salem were dark, darker than anything we experience today. Streets had no illumination except the cold white light of the moon and stars and whatever very dim glow might come from candlelit houses with their few windows. Even well-educated leaders living in Boston at the time were shaken by unusual sounds. Thunder, many felt, was a blast from God, a very personal judgment of New England. Yet in England, and soon in New England, some people were beginning to argue that storms were simply natural events. The dominant belief that God spoke as thunder and the newer view that sounds in the heavens had no special meaning were crossing each other in Salem Village, which only made for more tension and anxiety. For most residents of a jittery town, explaining night sounds and strange visions was getting easier and yet scarier: They were caused by witches among them, prowling, lurking, flying about, no longer hiding but attacking, even as the judges seemed to be rooting them out. Three obvious witches had been caught. Now the watch was on. Who was next?

Ann and the Putnam family had the answer, and, as would happen so often, they raised the stakes. The next witch Ann and her mother identified was no outsider, but a devout member of the Salem Village church. True, Martha Corey had borne a mixed-race, illegitimate child some years before, but there is no evidence that people continued to hold that past against her. Instead, Martha had the reputation of being a loyal churchgoer, a woman who took her religion seriously. Shortly after the Putnams accused Martha of being a witch, they named another. Rebecca Nurse was both the wife of a relatively wealthy man and a respected woman. She was, in fact, the very opposite of the usual image of a witch. It is as if the Putnams were focusing on a picture of the town, searching to find the face of evil; at first they selected outsiders, then a good woman with a past, then one of the best women of all. Though the Putnams themselves may not have been aware of it, to some historians the face Ann and her family wanted to find is quite obvious: that of Mary Veren Putnam, the evil stepmother who cost them their inheritance and perhaps their future.

Of TESTS
and wishes
Ann Jr. started the accusations, and the whole family—perhaps some of them reluctantly—joined her. Sometime around March 11, Ann broke the tense silence in Salem by announcing that the spirit of Martha Corey "did often appear to her and torture her by pinching and other ways." Ann's uncle Edward, who was a prominent member of the same church as Martha, and Ezekiel Cheever, the clerk who recorded the first examinations in this set of accusations, decided to investigate her charges. To be a member of a church in New England was a serious thing, and when a church member was accused of the vilest evil, the rest of her congregation had to weigh the claim carefully.

The two sober men decided to create a test that would challenge both Ann's vision of her tormentor and Martha's apparent godliness. They questioned Ann about what clothing Martha's evil specter was wearing. If Ann was sure she was being attacked by Martha, she would certainly be able to describe exactly what Martha looked like. And if Ann got the details right, Martha would be trapped. The invisible and the visible worlds seemed to be crossing and could be used to judge each other.

Ann was cunning and quick-thinking. She claimed that the specter had spoken clearly, naming itself as Martha, but had blinded the girl and refused to describe its clothes. This nimble defense preserved Ann's credibility with the judges and turned the test into a case of her word against Martha's. Martha also seemed to have heard about the test and was ready for the delegation. She smiled knowingly when they arrived at her home, saying, "I know what you are come for; you are come to talk with me about being a witch, but I am none. I cannot help people talking of me." This was the puzzled, confident voice of a person who would never expect to be accused of witchcraft. Martha knew who witches were. They were "idle, slothful persons" who "minded [obeyed] nothing that was good." And she challenged her questioners. Was her accuser able to describe her clothes? No answer. All eagerness, Martha pressed on. Could Ann say what she was wearing? Martha asked. When the two men reported Ann's excuse, a satisfied Martha gloated. She "seemed to smile at it as if she had showed us a pretty trick."

To Martha and to the eyes of history, a paper-thin accusation against a virtuous woman fell apart when confronted with the simplest challenges. But in Salem in March of 1692 there was a much darker way the same scene could be interpreted. Maybe Martha's smiles were not those of an innocent woman confident of having cleared her name, but those of a witch who knew exactly what would happen and had succeeded in covering her tracks.

When Martha went to visit Ann a few days after her interrogation, perhaps to personally reassure her, the young girl went wild. Choking, seemingly blinded, her hands and feet twisted in horrible ways, Ann told Martha to her face that "she did it." As Ann spoke, her tongue seemed pulled out of her mouth, and her teeth clamped down on it. When she could finally talk, Ann claimed to see a yellow bird suckling between Martha's fingers. The longer Martha stood there, the more fraught the situation became. Ann saw Martha's shade turning a spit in the fire, with a man roasting on it. Mercy Lewis, a servant in Ann's house, swung at the apparition with an iron rod. Soon Mercy, too, was in agony, as if the spirit were punishing her for attacking it. Though Martha was hustled away from the home, that night Mercy was "drawn toward the fire by unseen hands as she sat in a chair."

The judges heard two different versions of reality when Martha Corey was brought in for a hearing on March 21. Whom should they believe: a well-established

woman, defended by her reputation and her judgment,
or a cluster of accusers who seemed to meet any objec-
tion with ever more extreme behavior and accusations?
And the battle lines were drawn even more sharply by
then because of Abigail Williams, who, two days after
Martha's test, had claimed to be assaulted by the same
apparition that had attacked Ann. On March 19, Abigail
had another, more extreme fit, which, as we will soon
see, was similar to Mercy's in one key way. It was as if one
accuser was learning from another, creating an ever-
wilder scene for onlookers.

An important guest had arrived at Samuel Parris's
house on the night of March 19. The Reverend Deodat
Lawson, the former minister of Salem Village, had
returned to help in the village's time of trouble. As
Lawson saw it, Abigail was in the hands of a particularly
violent spirit. She was thrown back and forth across the
room. Like the Goodwin children, she seemed to
almost fly, "stretching her arms as high as she could,
and crying 'whish, whish, whish.'" Abigail began to
struggle with the shade of Rebecca Nurse, who was trying to force her to sign the dreaded book. "I won't, I
won't, I won't take it," she protested, fighting with the
air. Then, like Mercy Lewis, she ran to the fire, grabbed
at burning logs, and flung them into the room.

Abigail's words have come down to us as the weird
sounds of flight, something like "whoosh, whoosh,
whoosh." But perhaps she was actually saying something else. Maybe she and the other girls wished that

they could fly, that they could become like spirits, like free souls. The claim of the Quakers was that a person could experience the divine spirit directly. The girls might have heard of such beliefs, even as views condemned by elders. Perhaps the girls wanted the freedom to be as spirits themselves and resented the sober churchgoing adults who were their parents, as well as the people they accused. In acting out possession, perhaps they were showing a yearning for freedom. At the same time, though, they may have feared that the very inner impulses they wanted to let loose actually were demons seducing them and that every time they toyed with those spirits, they were blackening their souls. Abigail's "whish" suggests a mixture of desires that were making it difficult for young people either to fit into the roles demanded by their parents and their faith or to completely reject them.

This certainly seemed the case the next day, Sunday, when Lawson preached to his old congregation. Even as he spoke, some of the assembled began to have fits. Then, suddenly, Abigail interrupted and spoke out: "Now stand up, and name your text." The young girl was speaking in the voice of an adult male. Lawson began to read, and Abigail went a step further. "It is a long text," she complained. By all rights, an eleven- or twelve-year-old girl should be the most silent, most modest person in church. But by speaking as one afflicted by spirits, Abigail was emboldened to act not merely as an elder, but as a critic. In Salem

being afflicted by witches was now having very strange
results: It caused great pain, yet it also allowed victims
to speak freely. It was simultaneously agonizing and
liberating. Mrs. Bathshua Pope, an older woman who
had joined the brigade of accusers, saw her opportunity. As the sermon droned on she chimed in, "Now
there is enough of that."

The accusers were now working together, in force.
Martha Corey was in church that day, as she would
always be on a Sunday. But it soon appeared that there
was more than one Martha there. Abigail told everyone
to look up, for another Martha was seated high on a
beam, letting her yellow bird suckle between her fingers. Ann Putnam Jr. then joined in, seeing another
bird familiar on Lawson's own hat, which was resting on
a nail. The bird that Tituba introduced in her confession was appearing everywhere. If Tituba had been right
about the bird, what about the more terrifying aspects
of her confession—the man in black, the nine witches,
the evil spirits flying through the air? Soon they, too,
would appear in the visions of other accusers.

CHAPTER V

The One
and the
Many

...s for our Son Lord and Lady the Ki...
...That Sarah Buckley Wife of Willia...
In the County of Essex Shoom...
...he Eighteenth day of May
...aforesaid and divers other days an...
...as after Certaine detestable Arts
...uses Wickedly Mallitiously and feli...
...d and Exercised at and in the Tow...
...ty of Essex Aforesaid in t...
...ttman of Salom
...on by whi...
...hn Puttnam y Day & Yeare Afor...
...and times both before and after w...
...flicted Consumed Pined Wasted & ...
...ndry other Acts of Witchcraft b...
...kby Comittand done before
...t Our Son Lord and Lady the
...rowne & Dignity and the forme...

Martha
COREY

On Monday, March 21, Martha Corey was arrested on suspicion of witchcraft. Once again the people of Salem came out in force to witness her examination. How would a religious woman stand up against questioning? Could it really be that hidden in the very heart of the church was a servant of Satan?

Martha began by asking to pray. The ability to recite the Lord's Prayer perfectly was a basic test for witchcraft, as we saw in Cotton Mather's dealings with Goody Glover. So Martha was staking her claim from the start: *I am above suspicion, a devout woman,* she seemed to be saying. But Judge Hathorne was unmoved. Instead,

he challenged her again and again: "Why [do] you hurt
these persons?" He was like a prosecutor on a modern
TV show, attacking, badgering, provoking Martha,
trying to get her to slip up and reveal her true nature.
Though this is not the calm and fair approach we
expect of a judge, these hearings were not precisely trials. They were information-gathering sessions. The
judges had no more legal training than what they had
gained through life experience as leading men of their
community. Following the standard practice of the
day, they thought a tough, no-nonsense approach was
the best way to follow through on Tituba's confession
and get to the truth. As Hathorne put it in court, "We
came to be a terror to evil-doers." That made them
good at finding contradictions in testimony and completely unable to listen to anyone who fought back,
even through prayer.

Martha stood before the court and the community
stating what must have seemed to be simple truths
about herself: "I am an innocent person. I never had
to do with witchcraft since I was born. I am a Gospel
Woman." The chorus of the afflicted shot back, "A
Gospel Witch." Hathorne ignored Martha's claims
and proceeded to the issue of the clothes she was
wearing when the accusers saw her. How could she
know she would be questioned about that? the judge
asked. Martha stumbled. First she claimed her husband had warned her in advance. Then, when it was
revealed that he had denied doing this, she said she

knew the girls were talking about her and she expected
to be questioned.

In the verbal contest with the judge, Martha was
cracking. Just then the afflicted began to speak out.
There were at least ten of them by now, including four
adult women, three female servants, and the three girls
who had been at the center of the trouble from the
start, Betty Parris, Abigail Williams, and Ann Putnam
Jr. Most were in the meetinghouse listening. One girl
broke into the testimony: "There is a man whispering
in her [Martha's] ear."

"What did he say to you?" Hathorne questioned
the accused. "We must not believe all that these distracted children say," Martha replied, sounding very
much like a modern parent or teacher. To the court,
the fact that so many accusers made the same claims
suggested that they were telling the truth and that
Martha was lying. "You charge these children with distraction," Hathorne responded. "It is a note of distraction when persons vary in a minute, but these fix
upon you; this is not the manner of distraction." An
increasingly overwhelmed Martha could only answer,
"When all are against me, what [how] can I help it?"

In noting that the accusers were young—more pre-
teens, teenagers, and young women than what we
would now consider "children," but in the main not
yet full adults—Martha was appealing to the normal
standards of her community. An established churchgoing elder was much more trustworthy than a young

person, who was likely to be "distracted," fooled by emotions or fantasies. But this argument did Martha no good. Was it because the accusers were young and their suffering was so extreme that it caused judges, and the community at large, to put sympathy for their plight ahead of their usual judgment?

There was a kind of fury to the accusers' fits, which was probably more likely to be intimidating to doubters than productive of deep sympathy. But there was another sense in which the accusers' youth did figure in the trials. Witches were a kind of inversion of mothers—they fed foul pets with their evil breasts and were particularly suspect in the death of infants. John Milton was a devout English Puritan whose epic poem *Paradise Lost* was first published in 1667. In it he describes Hecate, queen of the witches, as "in secret, riding through the Air she comes / Lur'd with the smell of infant blood to dance with Lapland witches." In a community that was fearing for its political future and concerned that its powerfully held religious traditions were not being passed on to its young people, a witch, a demonic mother, was a kind of symbol of everything that endangered the future. The witch was a human given over to the devil, who was stealing children, possessing them, taking them away, just when they should be carrying on the faith. In this sense, anxiety about young people, an eagerness to protect and provide for them, may have overruled normal cautions.

It may even be, as Mary Beth Norton argues, that the young accusers were only believed when their accusations were supported by reports, now lost, written by adult males. If well-respected men observed the young accusers and reported that their fits were real, then the court would be heeding not just a girl, but an established man.

As at the Putnam house a few days before, during her visit with Ann, Martha's efforts to appear as a calm, devout woman clashed with the ever-rising extremes of the accusers' behavior. Every time Martha bit her lip, some of the afflicted women and girls would howl that they were being bitten and would insist on being examined to show the telltale marks. If Martha rubbed her hands together, as any nervous person might do while being questioned, more protests came from the audience and more demands to reveal the accusers' battered limbs. If Martha so much as leaned forward to rest on her seat, screams came from the crowd. It was as if good Martha Corey sitting in the meetinghouse were a shell of a person, while her evil shade floated above the crowd, pulling at her puppet victims on invisible strings. Or, seen from her perspective, it was as if the crowd were a sea of anger and hatred rising and crashing against one lone individual. The truth of the crowd versus that of the individual was a recurring issue in the Salem trials.

Feeding off of one another, the accusers were like a pack of wild animals, one darting ahead with some

aggressive behavior and the others rushing in to follow her lead. Mrs. Pope screamed that her very bow-
els were being torn out by the witch, and she began to
throw things at Martha. Then others started hurling
accusations at Martha, as if they were the judges
directing the testimony. Why wasn't Martha out with
the other witch spirits who were gathering in front of
the meetinghouse? Didn't she hear the drum beating,
calling her? Wasn't the man in black right there, whispering in her ear? Wasn't the yellow bird drinking its
evil juice from between her fingers that very move-

ment? The judges quickly looked to
see if there was any evidence of suckling marks on Martha's hands, but
the accusing girl said it was too late.
Martha had already spirited away a
pin—perhaps to draw blood for the
bird?—and it was found "sticking
upright" out of Martha's head.

What can we make of these bites
and scars and black-and-blue marks
and, especially, the pin? Pins kept
coming up in the trials. In a later
hearing Ann Putnam Jr. would claim
that the specter of one accused witch,

Though it no longer exists, this bottle was said to hold
pins that had been kept as evidence after they appeared
during the Salem trials and pretrial hearings.
According to the very knowledgable Danvers town
archivist Richard B. Trask, the shape of the pins shown
here dates from the seventeenth century, so they may
well have been actual relics from the trials.

Elizabeth How, stuck a pin in Ann's hand even as Elizabeth herself was being questioned. Years later the Reverend Lawson reported that these pins appeared in the wrists and arms of the afflicted and that in one case an accuser "had a pin run through both her upper and lower lip when she was called to speak." He also claimed that invisible forces were able to bind up their victims with real ropes and, in some cases, even hang them on hooks from which they had to be cut down. One accuser, Susannah Sheldon, apparently was bound four times in two weeks by two evil spirits and had to be cut free repeatedly by friends and neighbors.

The wounds are one of the defining issues in the whole Salem story. To the most skeptical, these injuries and props are the clearest signs of a conspiracy. If someone shows up at a legal hearing with a pin stuck in her hand or through her lip, it must have been put there intentionally. The accusers would not have so confidently asked to display their wounds unless they knew they were there—especially because they claimed, and apparently the court agreed, that the wounds matched the teeth patterns of the accused. To get even an approximate match to a bite pattern requires having a handy means of faking very particular scars. And no one is bound up with a thick cord and left to dangle on a hook by accident.

Staging events such as these takes planning. According to the critic Robert Calef, in one case the accusers were actually caught trying to use faked evidence in court. During the trial of Sarah Good one accuser claimed to have been stabbed by the witch's spirit form, and she produced the broken knife to prove it. But a young man testified that he had accidentally broken that very knife the day before and threw it away in a place near the accuser. The court criticized the accuser for lying but did not go on to question the rest of her testimony. The many mentions of bites and pins suggest that this kind of fraud happened frequently—unless you believe the accusers' claims that evil ghosts were flying around Salem doing their worst.

Martha Corey had no reason to bring a pin to the hearing to indict herself. It seems possible that as the crowd heated up, with people egging one another on, accusers made use of everything they saw around them. If Martha had a pin in her hair, suddenly it became a pin removed from her hand. There were no cameras to record what she looked like when she arrived. If someone waved a scratched arm in the dark room of the meetinghouse, how carefully could it be examined? There were no dental records to check. What people expected to see may well have been what they saw.

No one aside from Lawson—twelve years after the events in Salem, when his own life was going poorly and he had every reason to want to justify his role in the trials—reported the most extreme cases involving ropes and pins. The accusers who most closely matched Lawson by claiming to have repeatedly found Susannah Sheldon tied up also testified that brooms and poles were whisked out of their houses by spirits and left in nearby trees. The strangeness of the claims makes it hard to judge them. After all, it is hard to believe that someone came to a hearing with a pin stuck through her lips and no one noticed, or that she jabbed it in at some later time without attracting any attention. Even the broken knife seems like a prop picked up at the last moment, not part of a carefully planned strategy.

However they got there, the wounds and pins are important as a sign of the increasing boldness—or perhaps consuming mania—of the accusers. Abigail interrupted a sermon and mocked a minister; Mrs. Pope threw things in the middle of a solemn hearing; someone risked claiming a pin had magically appeared in court; the bite marks were flaunted so often, the accusers must have been very confident that they would be convincing; the man in black joined the yellow bird in migrating from Tituba's confession into common reference.

When questioned by a doubter, one of the girls later said there was nothing to the accusations: "[I] did it for sport, [we] must have some sport." If that is how it began, the game was now completely out of control. The accusers either were carrying out a malicious plot that drew in more and more conspirators or were in a highly charged state of mind in which each backed up and further excited the others. There was no truth except their passion to be heard and their drive to expand their range of destruction.

"Confess and give GLORY to GOD"

"Confess and give GLORY to GOD" If Martha Corey was the test case of the accusers' power, Rebecca Nurse was the proof. There was a bit of gossip about Rebecca: Her mother had once been accused of being a witch. Though that case never went to court, many believed witchcraft ran in families, which made Rebecca more vulnerable to accusations. And there is a record of conflict over a neighbor's pigs wandering onto her land that might suggest Rebecca had an argumentative streak. But Rebecca was also known as an active, devout church member. According to her friends and supporters, when she was first told that the accusers were mentioning her, she said she grieved for the Reverend Parris

The Nurse family lived on three hundred acres of land in this area, and Francis Nurse prospered. This home probably was built not long after Rebecca Nurse was tried and convicted. It is not hard to picture a house such as this as a boat, an ark planted on land.

and his family in their afflictions. "She pitied them with all her heart," even though she herself was frail and ill. She was said to be equally humble in her acceptance of God's will and her concern for others, even her accusers.

For the Putnams, Rebecca Nurse's good reputation may have been hard to take. Her husband had worked himself up from nothing to become a substantial farmer. He prospered by his own efforts during the very years of the Putnams' frustrations and disappointments. Then he joined with the Salem Town leaders who opposed the family in the struggles over the choice of a minister for Salem Village. In many ways, then, Rebecca was a perfect symbol of the forces threatening the Putnams and their ways. She was as close as they could come to Mary Veren Putnam without naming her. In court it would be decided which brand of Puritanism would rule in Salem: the self-made individual speaking for herself or the vengeful clan with the ever-growing support of the community.

This time it was the elder Ann Putman who led the attack. On Wednesday of that busy third week in March, Deodat Lawson returned to visit the Putnams. Ann Sr. was in a bad way, apparently under spectral attack at the very moment of his visit, and she asked the reverend to pray with her. Her symptoms were similar to those suffered by one of the Goodwin children: She was so stiff, "she could not be bended." Once she could move, her legs and arms flailed about, as if she were fighting someone off. "Goodwife Nurse, be gone! Be gone! Be gone!" she demanded. Ann and the invisible spirit then began a furious argument. "I know, I know what will make you afraid: the wrath of angry God. I am sure that will make you afraid. Be gone, do not torment me. I know what you would have, but it is out of your reach. It is clothed with the white robes of Christ's righteousness," Ann cried.

Lawson assumed that what the specter wanted, and what Ann was fighting to protect, was her soul. But if, as one set of historians has argued, Rebecca Nurse really stood for Mary Veren Putnam and all the successful Salem Town people who were rising as the Putnams suffered in Salem Village, then a very different battle was raging in Ann's confused mind. Yelling "I know what you would have" was Ann screaming at those sneaky, evil people who seemed to her to be stealing from her family without ever being stopped. Was she pleading with them not to take everything? If this interpretation is true, then to the agony-racked Putnam household, the spirit of Rebecca Nurse threatened to erase all the family had built. Yet other scholars think that there is far too little evidence to engage in this kind of speculation about the inner meaning of Ann's cries. Whatever Ann Sr.'s motives were, the damage was done. Rebecca Nurse would have to speak for herself in court.

The scene was always the same: the group against the individual. Judge Hathorne respected Goodwife Nurse as he had no previous prisoner and spoke to her with care and consideration. But first Abigail and

Ann Jr. testified against her. Rebecca responded, "I can say before my Eternal Father I am innocent, and God will clear my innocency." The judge offered Rebecca a path to rejoining the group, saying everyone there hoped she was truly innocent, "but if you be guilty, pray God discover [expose] you." *Confess and come back,* he seemed to plead. *Don't stand against us; don't force us to convict you.*

As Tituba's case had shown, an accused witch who confessed was no longer of interest to the accusers or the court. She or he was put in jail, but there were no immediate further punishments. Although, in the end, all the confessed witches risked being executed, that ultimate fate would come in the future, whereas confessing would end the heated clash in court.

Just then a man in the crowd jumped in, saying that when Rebecca had come into his house recently, he had felt something weird. Three to one. And the crowd was itching to get involved, throwing words the way a lynch mob might throw stones.

Ann Sr. began to speak, if speaking it was, for she was in a battle for her life. She felt she was being ripped apart by ferocious beasts, in "the paws of those roaring lions and the jaws of those tearing bears." "Did you not bring the Black Man with you?" she demanded of the defendant. "Did you not bid me tempt God and die?" Ann spat out before being so overcome that she had to be carried out of the courtroom. But by now at least three others were screaming, wailing, and falling to the floor. Once again the accused witch seemed to be a puppet master, for every motion Rebecca made had a sick reflection in more and more people being bitten, pinched, bruised, and tormented, howling as if their backs were being broken. The roaring of the crowd built and built, until Lawson, passing by outside, heard the "hideous screech and noise." The count was over. It was all against one. No one could tell anymore who was witch and who was saint, who was accuser and who was accused, except that one woman was before them being questioned and everyone else was in the mob against her. "The whole assembly was struck with consternation, and they were afraid that those that sat next to them were under the influence of witchcraft."

Hathorne, barely able to be heard, tried to mediate. "Do you not see what a solemn condition these are in?" he offered, translating, as it were, from the mob to the victim. *Give me a way,* he seemed to be saying, *to calm them and save you.* But the crowd was not in a mood for forgiveness. Two more people rose up to display their afflictions.

Rebecca Nurse had nothing new to say. "The Lord knows I have not hurt them. I am an innocent person."

The drama now had three sides: the wild crowd, the imploring judge, the solitary accused. Hathorne began almost to plead with Rebecca to see her way out: "Confess and give glory to God." Rebecca refused. "It is all false, I am clear," and she rejected every overture he made. Until, at the very end of the day, she finally understood the deal the judge wanted to make and responded directly to his offer: "Would you have me belie myself?"

The Puritan conscience would tolerate no lies. Being true to herself, Rebecca Nurse could not take the judge's bargain. But in the Salem meetinghouse a different side of the Puritan experience now ruled: the consensus of the group. Confession had always been the very worst thing to do in a witchcraft case, a sure path to being executed. Now it was something else, a way to accept the judgment of the community and join its cause. What Tituba figured out how to do for herself was now a role available to anyone: "Confess and give glory to God."

Rebecca was held for further examination. The Reverend Lawson was not in the room to witness her testimony because he had a sermon to prepare. He was to come in after the day's hearings and speak. No one could miss the growing passions of the mob nor quite ignore the questions the accused kept raising. Like Sarah Osborne, Rebecca Nurse objected that "I cannot help it, the Devil may appear in my shape." In other words, evil could appear in any form it chose—including that of an innocent person. This was a very serious issue, for the entire weight of the evidence against the accused lay in the ghostly attacks that seemed to be spreading across Salem. Any serious thinker and leader of the community had to analyze evidence that was subject to so many questions and yet seemed tied to such undeniably terrifying behavior. On the afternoon of March 24, facing a crowd barely recovered from its convulsions, the Reverend Lawson had his turn.

Lawson was a rather ineffectual minister who had a sad history with Salem, for his wife and a daughter had died there. He gave a well-meaning, contradictory sermon that offered no clear advice but to "pray, pray, pray." Sounding a bit like John Goodwin, he urged his former congregation to understand that they had brought these ills on themselves. He knew firsthand about the "fires of contention" that divided Salem Town and Salem Village, for those disputes had cost him his job. But he did not take the next step of directly challenging the accusers. After all, they were the very people who had supported him. Instead, he first warned that the devil was eager to sign up followers and to "use their bodies and minds, shapes and representations, to affright and afflict others." Then he backed off by arguing that the devil would not be able to appear in the form of the truly saved. *Be careful,* he seemed to say, *mind your own sins. But, yes, the evil spirits could well be among us.*

One minister was ineffectual. The other was all too clear. Three days later the Reverend Samuel Parris, in whose very home the whole crisis had begun, gave his opinion. He took as his theme Jesus' knowledge that one of his twelve closest followers was a betrayer. Parris was telling his congregation that even the most seemingly

pious person, even a very pillar of the community, could
be in league with the devil. In this he was agreeing with
the accusations against Martha Corey and Rebecca
Nurse. "Christ knows," he warned, "how many Devils
among us, wither [whether] one or ten or twenty!"
Parris did not think the devil could use the spirit of a
truly good person. But his sermon answered that question by avoiding it. Since everyone—everyone sitting
next to you, everyone praying with you in church, everyone you have ever known and trusted—might well be
infected with evil, what did it matter that the devil could
use only the specters of those he had corrupted?
Corruption, rot, and evil had penetrated everywhere.

Parris was the first pastor to have the Salem Village
church as his own, no longer tied to Salem Town. He
did not let down his supporters. The leading edge of
evil, he said, was the "lust of covetousness." Men now
"prefer farms and merchandise above" God and his
laws. If the Putnams were searching for the face of evil
in their own family nightmares, Parris named as the
source of witchcraft the very kind of business success
that was distinguishing Salem Town. According to its
minister, Salem Village's challenge was not so much to
carefully weigh dubious evidence as to be on hyper
alert, to suspect all, and to fight back against evils
everywhere. If he did not specifically endorse the mob
scene in the meetinghouse, he urged his listeners to be
even more ferocious in the future.

As the reverend's words thundered from the pulpit,

Rebecca Nurse's sister Sarah Cloyce got up and walked out, flinging the door shut behind her. Or was it that the wind slammed the door against its frame? Was she an angry woman, frustrated at the minister's harsh tone? Or was she a witch exposed by a probing sermon? The accusers had no doubt, and soon the young regulars, joined by John Indian and two other men, began to file complaints against Sarah. It was clear now that at least in Salem Village the crowd, supported by its minister, was in charge.

CHAPTER VI

From Hearings
TO TRIALS

...s for our Sov^r Lord and Lady the K...

That Sarah Buckley Wife of Willia...

In the County of Essex Shoom...

...he Eighteenth day of May — —

...aforesaid and divers other days an...

...as after ...ertaine detestable Arts...

...s Wickedly Malitiously and fell...

...d and Exercised at and in the Tou...

...ty of Essex — — aforesaid in...

...ttman of Salem — — —

...n — — — — — by whi...

...hn Puttnam ye Day & Yeare aford...

...nd times both before and after w...

...ricked Consumed Pined Wasted & ...

...ndry other Acts of Witchcraft by...

...bly — — ...omitted and done before...

...st our Sov^r Lord and Lady the...

...rowne & Dignity and the forme...

"Alas, alas, alas, WITCHCRAFT"

Five people had been arrested for witchcraft. At least one more obvious suspect had been uncovered, and a whole town was inflamed. The leaders of New England realized that they would have to deal with the crisis in Salem Village. But who would those leaders be? Increase Mather was due back from England shortly with a new governor, bringing new laws for the colony. Until the ship carrying them docked, New England was in a strange kind of limbo. It had officials and courts, all of English law. It had sixty years of its own laws and cases to consult, as well as learned ministers, such as Cotton Mather, to give advice. And yet it had no certainty over what new rules might arrive with the tide.

The prosecution of Sarah Cloyce quickly yielded new suspects, including Elizabeth Proctor, the wife of John Proctor and the central figure in Arthur Miller's famous play *The Crucible*. Sarah and Elizabeth were two more well-respected churchgoing women similar to Martha Corey and Rebecca Nurse, and doubts and resentments about those being accused began to be openly expressed in Salem. In time a large group of petitioners would approach the court in defense of Rebecca, and there were mutterings of disbelief as rumors went round about Elizabeth. Nevertheless, the next hearing was scheduled for April 11, and this time Judges Hathorne and Corwin would have a distinguished panel of five judges to sit with them, including the deputy governor of New England, Thomas Danforth, and the devout, learned merchant Samuel Sewall. Inasmuch as New England had political leadership, these men were there to see for themselves what was really going on in Salem.

Danforth tried something new. Instead of questioning the accused, leaving it to the crowd to take its cues from the flow of talk and pick its moment to attack, he spoke directly to the accusers. It was up to them to state what they had experienced and then have the accused respond. Now the accusers would have to speak as individuals, too. This tactic did change the mood in the courtroom for a while, but due to a twist of fate, it had only limited effect. For the first person Danforth questioned was John Indian, and like his wife, Tituba, he knew his part. John had no trouble indicting Sarah and Elizabeth, even when Sarah shot back her own challenge, "Oh, you are a grievous liar."

The other accusers started out carefully, responding to questions but not taking over the meeting. One had a fit, but it did not spread. Another reported that she had seen about forty witches meeting—thirty-one more than Tituba had seen listed in the devil's book— and that Sarah and Elizabeth were like deacons in their anti-church. A third elaborated on a variation in the visions of evil. Mercy Lewis had seen "a white man" "in a glorious place" who led a "great multitude in white glittering robes." Mercy's image was very like those in Scripture, yet somehow the opposite, for this was the devil, not God. Mary Walcott told the judges that she had seen him too, "a great many times," and that he "made all the witches to tremble." The story was building now, the accusers gaining confidence that even with these important men in the room, they could hold the stage. Mixing angels and devils in a vision of "glittering robes" may have been what court was like for the accusers: They could scream and yell, they could seem to fly, they could see sacred sights, even if doing this destroyed the lives and reputations of their neighbors. And no one would stop them.

Perhaps Sarah Cloyce sensed the changing mood, for she asked for some water and then slumped in her chair in a faint. That was the signal for chaos to break loose. Now the fits spread across the afflicted, and the visions followed. They saw Sarah's spirit flying off to prison to join "her sister Nurse." In a moment the waves of fits, cries, bites, and screams would crest, silencing the doubting judges and damning the accused.

"Elizabeth Proctor," Danforth's voice thundered out, "speak the truth." He broke the spell of the moment. He made sure Elizabeth knew the gravity of the charges, but he also would not let the accusers take over. He went back to questioning accused and accusers one by one.

"Speak the truth," he demanded of Mary Walcott. "You must speak the truth, as you will answer it before God another day. Mary Walcott! Does this woman hurt you?"

"I never saw her so as to be hurt by her," Mary answered meekly.

"Mary [Mercy] Lewis! Does she hurt you?" Silence.

"Ann Putnam, does she hurt you?" Silence.

"Abigail Williams, does she hurt you?" Silence— her hand was thrust in her own mouth.

"John! Does she hurt you?"

"This is the woman that came in her shift [nightgown] and choked me," John insisted. And he revived the crowd. Like Tituba, John must have known there was only one way out for a slave being questioned by a master: Create a story that worked, insist on it, elaborate on it, and find allies.

John's confidence spread. Soon Ann Jr. was back in action, sure that Elizabeth hurt her. The fits began again.

"Abigail Williams! Does this woman hurt you?"

"Yes, sir, often."

Danforth's efforts to challenge the accusers had almost worked, and then it had collapsed.

Elizabeth Proctor tried to remonstrate with her accusers by reminding them, as Danforth had done, of God. "Dear child . . . there is another judgment, dear child," she pleaded. She was answered with convulsions and screams from the accusers. And now the visions came back, stronger than ever. Now Elizabeth's husband, John Proctor, was sitting up in the beams, a vile wizard. He was about to attack Mrs. Pope. Suddenly, her feet flew up in the air.

"[Goodwife,] what do you say . . . to these things?"

"I know not, I am innocent."

The courtroom was a scene of rising hysteria. John Proctor's spirit was on the loose, going after another accuser, and as one noticed him, the other screamed. A man rose to testify that he had just seen the spirits of both Proctors along with other known witches in his room. Completely confident, the two young girls, Ann Putnam Jr. and Abigail Williams, walked up to Elizabeth Proctor and swung at her, only to have their fists blocked by her spirit. As Abigail's fingers trailed against Elizabeth's clothes, it seemed her fingertips sizzled, as if burned. Abigail cried out, and Ann collapsed.

A day that had begun with doubting judges and the leaders of the colony coming to test a local issue ended with the crowd triumphant. Not only had they succeeded in bringing down two more enemies, in court, under the eyes of the judges, but they had also attacked a third. Samuel Sewall was convinced. "'Twas awful to see how the afflicted persons were agitated," he wrote. He later added, "*Vae* [alas], *vae, vae,* witchcraft."

There was no doubt about the law in Salem; it was the rule of the pack.

To hear and
DECIDE
By the time Sir William Phips, the new governor of the Massachusetts Bay Colony, arrived in Boston on May 14, twenty-seven accused witches were housed in Boston jails. To gain control of the colony, Phips had to deal with the cases at once. "The prisons," he later wrote to England, were "full of people committed upon suspicion of witchcraft." Born in Maine, Phips grew up in the New World and made his reputation as a fighter and scavenger for sunken Spanish ships. The Puritan leadership could hardly have asked for a governor more different from his predecessor, the hated Sir Edmond Andros. Yet Phips was not a strong political leader. He seems to have been more concerned with pleasing strong factions in England and New England, and then protecting his own reputation, than in tackling the serious issues raised by the witchcraft trials.

William Stoughton, the ambitious judge who led the new court of Oyer and Terminer.

Phips found a colony that was "miserably harassed with a most horrible witchcraft." To remedy the situation, he ruled—hastily if not surprisingly—that convicted witches would be executed, and he asked nine leading men to function as the court of Oyer and Terminer [Hearing and Determining] to hold the trials. He named the respected minister and judge William Stoughton as the chief justice and then created a panel that included Hathorne and Corwin, to ensure continuity; four prominent merchants, including Samuel Sewall; a doctor; and a military man. Though actual decisions would be made by juries, the judges would have a decisive influence on the trials.

Almost immediately, the undertow of doubt about the cases that was surfacing in Salem conversations made itself felt in the new court. Nathaniel Saltonstall was one of the judges appointed to the new

Samuel Sewall confirmed that there were witches and helped to sit judgment over them. But his conscience continued to bother him after the end of the trials, and he ultimately asked forgiveness for the sin of having been part of the court that hanged witches.

court. An experienced judge and politician, he decided to interview one of the accused witches himself. Her name was Rachel Clinton, and the evidence against her included the kind of strange stories that make these cases read like fairy tales. Thomas Boarman claimed that one night when Rachel was under suspicion, he saw something like a cat, which changed into a little dog. As he chased after the creature in the dark, it managed always to stay the same distance ahead, until suddenly Thomas saw something like a giant turtle running rapidly beside him. The minute he thought of Rachel, both the scampering, shape-changing spirit dog and the speedy tortoise disappeared. Faced with evidence such as this, Saltonstall objected to the charges against three of the women, perhaps sat in on the first trial, and then resigned altogether from the new court.

Saltonstall's speedy exit from the trials shows that powerful people were skeptical about the accusations from very early on. However compelling the accusers might have been when gathered in a meetinghouse, however loudly the local ministers proclaimed that a great evil was afoot in Salem, another voice was making itself heard in Massachusetts. It belonged to those who found no messages in thunder, nothing remarkable in the fears of a man battling night shadows on a dark road, and nothing compelling about howling, bleeding, fainting accusers. Even as young women were claiming to be knocked down by the evil eyes of witches, skeptics were questioning by what laws of

physics that could be possible. The racket in Salem can
be seen as an effort by a majority attached to its folkways, magical beliefs, and religious faith to drown out
a very modern-sounding, doubting voice that
belonged to a small minority—a voice that nonetheless
was already too strong to be ignored.

Even the most devout ministers saw themselves as
highly rational men and were troubled by the kind of
evidence being used in Salem. When another justice
turned to Cotton Mather for guidance in the coming
cases, Mather took a guarded, cautious line. If spirits
were attacking people, he wrote, it was certainly possible that devils were at fault, not the accused witches.
This was exactly what Sarah Osborne and Rebecca
Nurse had said in court. And as we have seen, this
contradiction lay at the heart of the whole Salem case
from the beginning. Why accept the results of the rye
cake test if it made use of the devil's power? Why trust
evil ghosts to give away their true nature? Still, Mather
could not entirely dismiss what seemed like overwhelming evidence of witchcraft. He suggested using
spectral evidence as a kind of hint, a warning, a scent
of evil that would have to be confirmed by tough questioning, by examining the accused for telltale signs
that they suckled their familiars, and ultimately—
ideally—by a valid confession.

One of the tragedies of Salem may have been that
great ministers like Cotton Mather were in an impossible
bind, for they believed in reason *and* in witchcraft. As the

accusations mounted, they faced an ever more difficult choice with ever-higher stakes: Follow your reasoning mind and challenge the clearest outbreak of demonic evil New England had ever faced; or follow your faith and perhaps consign innocent people to death.

One dead:

bridget BISHOP
The first case to be heard by the new court was the easiest. Bridget Bishop had a reputation for witchcraft that went back at least twenty years. Like Sarah Good, she was exactly the kind of person who was brought frequently to trial on witchcraft charges but who, previously, had generally gone free for lack of good evidence. When Judge Hathorne pressed Bridget to confess, she responded with the kind of defiance that had helped her and other accused witches in the past. "I am not here to say I am a witch [which would mean that you would] . . . take away my life." That was now exactly the wrong approach to take.

Seven years earlier, at least according to the new testimony they gave, two men who were tearing down a house Bridget used to live in had found rag puppets with pins stuck in them hidden in the walls. Like what we call "voodoo dolls," these puppets were the tools witches were known to use to harm people at a distance. For historians who believe there were actual witches in Salem, this is a key piece of evidence. But others question why the workers didn't mention such a startling discovery earlier, when they had the pup-

**From Hearings
to Trials**

pets on hand to submit as evidence, and they point
out that the hearing records are full of old rumors,
some stretching back twenty years, which people
dredged up whenever a neighbor was accused of
witchcraft. When Bridget's body was examined in private, experienced women found clear evidence of the
oddly formed extra breast witches developed to feed
their familiars. Though a second search produced the
opposite result, no one asked to reconcile the two
tests. Instead, people practically lined up to testify to
having been magically hurt by Bridget.

For all the evidence drawn from village gossip, the
crux of the case was still the tortures of the afflicted. As
the new court had been gathering, the behavior of the
afflicted had been, if anything, turning more extreme.
John Indian had a fit while riding with someone on
horseback. He clamped his teeth on the neck of the
poor man sitting in front of him, wailing that a ghostly
Bridget Bishop was attacking with a stick.

The stakes rose again in court. Ann Putnam Jr. and
Abigail Williams had opened up new possibilities for the
accusers by seeming to be struck down when they
approached Elizabeth Proctor. They no longer had to
claim there was a specter present doing her bidding. Now,
it seemed, the evil forces flowed directly from the person
seated in front of them. According to Cotton Mather's
later report, at Bridget's trial "she did but cast her eyes on
them, they were presently [immediately] struck down; and
this in such a manner as there could be no collusion in the

business." A witch, it now appeared, could use her evil vision to knock down her accusers. But she, and only she, could also heal them. "Upon the touch of her hand upon them, when they lay in their swoon they would immediately revive." Bridget's evil eye worked even when there were no victims to respond to it. Under guard of her jailers, she glanced at the meetinghouse that hosted so many hearings, something crashed, and a board filled with nails materialized in a new space. Or at least that is what Mather reported. It might have been a windy day in May, too.

Judge Stoughton's charge to the jury showed how the justices filtered the demonstrations they had seen through their experience in law and the advice they had received from Cotton Mather. According to Thomas Brattle, a critic who lived through the trials and most clearly expressed the rational, skeptical point of view, Stoughton completely ignored all caution. The judge specifically said that it did not matter whether the supposed victims actually experienced the afflictions they so loudly demonstrated in court, so long as they were suffering from something that "*tended* to their being pined and consumed, wasted, etc." The judge confirmed the rule of the majority. So long as many people were visibly miserable, so long as one fit confirmed another, it did not matter that one person exaggerated a bit or that another screamed just to be heard or that a third used a broken knife as a prop. Something was wrong, and it was likely enough that the accused witch was responsible.

Following these instructions, then, the jury con-

victed Bridget Bishop. She was pronounced the first
official witch in Salem, and on June 10 she was executed.

One dead, twenty-six in prison. This was a serious, and ominous, moment. The leading ministers of
the colony, led by both Increase and Cotton Mather,
could not let the executions go on without taking a
stand on the evidence. "The Return of Several
Ministers," which they published on June 15, was the
very opposite of what we might expect from Puritan
leaders. They were completely against the noise,
clamor, and chaos of the hearings, they wrote. They
did not trust victims who claimed to be knocked down
by a witch's glance or healed by her touch. They
specifically rejected the test of reciting the Lord's
Prayer that Cotton himself had used with Goody
Glover. Finally and firmly, they settled the question
of spectral evidence: "It is an undoubted and notorious thing that a demon may, by God's permission,
appear, even to ill purposes, in the shape of an innocent, yea, and a virtuous man." Speaking with one
voice, the most serious, most devout, and most
learned men in the colony dismissed the conduct and
the main evidence of the witchcraft trials.

The Salem witch crisis could have ended there,
with Bridget Bishop its one victim. But the ministers
were perhaps feeling their way with a new government. They ended their statement with a last paragraph that left the court on its own. Be careful, they
warned, but finish up what you have started: "We . . .

humbly recommend unto the government the speedy and vigorous prosecution of such as have rendered themselves obnoxious, according to the direction given in the laws of God, and the wholesome statutes of the English nation, for the detection of witchcraft."

And so, by midsummer of 1692, the Salem crisis was starting to splinter the Massachusetts colony into five distinct camps and one group not yet heard from. First, in Salem, there was the growing clan of accusers and second, one by one, the lonely voices of the accused. Thirdly, there was the voice of the government, expressed by the judges of the court of Oyer and Terminer and led by Judge Stoughton, which read English law as confirming the validity of the wild fits, even if they were questionable in some details. Fourth were the ministers, wavering, having real doubts about the evidence, but unwilling to stand against a concept of witchcraft that they believed in and a government they were eager to influence. And finally, there were the clear-eyed doubters, the Nathaniel Saltonstalls, Thomas Brattles, and Robert Calefs, who saw nothing in the trials but superstition, melodrama, and the destruction of innocent victims. The one faction not yet heard from were those successful merchants—the Salem Town leaders and their peers in Boston—who would soon see the accusations of their enemies coming closer and closer to them.

Supported by the court, the accusers were the most

confident force. It is possible that this surge was fed by the ever-greater involvement of accusers, such as Mercy Lewis, who had experienced the horrors of the Indian wars in Maine. Many of the judges had been responsible for botched campaigns and other military failures in that region. If screaming young people were able to point out demons in human form who might be seen as the cause of the colony's insecure borders, those judges would be only too likely to agree. And, just now, the Salem pack was racing toward its moment of triumph.

CHAPTER VII

The Man in Black

...s for our Sov[n] Lord and Lady the Ki...
...that Sarah Buckley Wife of Willia...

In the County of Essex Shoom...
...he Eighteenth day of May — —
...d aforesaid and divers other days an...
...as after certaine detestable Arts
...corist Wickedly Mallitiously and fel...
...d and Exercised at and in the To...
...nty of Essex — — aforesaid in ...
...attman of Salem
...an — — — — — by whi...
...hn Puttnam y[e] Day & Yeare afo...
...and times both before and after ...
...flicted Consumed Pined Wasted ...
...undry other Acts of Witchcraft b...
...kley — Committed and done before
...st Our Sov[n] Lord and Lady the
...rowne & Dignity and the form...

Vengeful
GHOSTS
According to young Ann Putnam's testimony, the most frightening night in her life must have been May 5, when the specter of former minister George Burroughs returned to her, followed by the spirits of his first two wives. Burroughs had first appeared to her fifteen days earlier, and it was a terrifying visitation, even for Ann. "What, are ministers witches too?" she cried out. Ann addressed the specter of the minister-gone-bad in the voice of the horrified community. "I told [him] it was a dreadful thing, that he . . . [who was] a minister [who] should teach children to fear God should [instead] come to

persuade poor creatures to give their souls to the devil."

The spirit admitted he was Burroughs and that he had "bewitched" his first two wives to death. Indeed, he was responsible for the deaths of Reverend Lawson's wife and daughter.

Based on Ann's word and many other similar spirit sightings, Burroughs was arrested in his new home, the town that is now called Wells, Maine, and brought back to Salem. He arrived on May 4.

The very next night the whole grim family—the wizard Burroughs and the ghosts of his two avenging victims—was back in Ann's room.

The ghastly wives "turned their faces towards Mr. Burroughs and looked very red and angry and told him that he had been a cruel man to them and that their blood did cry for vengeance against him." The wronged women cursed Burroughs, saying they would ascend to heaven and wear white robes, while he would be "cast into hell." Hearing this, he disappeared, and they remained to tell Ann their horrifying story. When they looked directly at her, Ann could see their eerie, pale faces, and they revealed that Burroughs had murdered both of them. He had stabbed the first one under her arm and covered the wound on the corpse with sealing wax. The ghostly form removed her shroud to show "the place."

This first wife had lived with Burroughs when he was the minister in Salem and had lived in the very home the Reverend Parris now occupied. Both wives demanded that Ann speak up for them to the judges in front of Burroughs. While Ann did not say this directly, she may have been referring to the common belief at the time that "murder will out"—that the signs of a terrible crime would appear magically. Perhaps she was suggesting that all the weird occult events that centered on the Parris household were a result of these spirits wanting their story to be told and demanding justice be done to Burroughs.

Ever since Tituba mapped out the conspiracy of evil, one figure stood out as the mastermind: the man in black. He was the devil, who held the book inscribed with the names of the damned and led the satanic meetings. If Ann's mother was struggling with images of respected women, trying to bring into focus a face she could never quite see, the younger Ann was aiming at an even more important and frightening figure. George Burroughs, former minister of Salem Village, a man who had lived with his first wife in the Putnams' own home the year Ann was born, was the closest human counterpart to the devil himself.

Burroughs was one of six names the judges heard on April 30. This was clearly a new phase of the outbreak. For among the accused was Philip English, the richest man in Salem, the owner of twenty-one ships and fourteen buildings. In mid-May yet another wealthy male was named, Daniel Andrew of Salem Town. Daniel was married to John Porter's youngest daughter and was a constant opponent of the Putnams

A nineteenth-century drawing of Philip English's substantial home. He was the wealthiest person in Salem to be accused of witchcraft.

in town politics. Naming him was as close as the Salem Village clan ever came to directly attacking the family that haunted them. At the end of the month John Alden, the son of the famous John Alden of Plymouth Colony and a wealthy sea captain and seasoned soldier in his own right, was added to the list.

The accusations coming from Salem were now far outside any previous pattern of witchcraft allegations: not just women, but men; not just poor local people disliked for being angry or resented for their neediness, but leaders of the community. Until recently, historians saw this last group of accusations as a sign that the witch-hunt was spinning out of control. But according to Mary Beth Norton, there were clear and logical reasons for accusing these wealthy and powerful people. Accusers who had lived through bloody Indian attacks in Maine could recall gossip and rumors that pinpointed each of these people as betrayers who were responsible for their torments.

Still, most of these new suspects were treated carefully. English and his wife, Mary, who was also named by the afflicted, were allowed to leave their jail cells during the day, so long as they returned at night.

Andrew was loosely guarded. It was far from clear how these cases would play out. Burroughs was another matter. The stories about him literally set people's ears "tingling." With him, evil itself was coming to trial.

Two MEN
in BLACK
The Reverend Burroughs seems to have been a short man with a black beard, proud of his physical strength, and given to doing things his own way. And then there was the matter of his clothing. As a minister, he wore a black coat. The "man in black," a minister wearing black: What is black and holy can also be black and evil.

On the evening of May 7 the servant Mercy Lewis met his spirit. Like a good pastor, it had a book to show her. Yet this was unlike any book she had seen when she worked for Burroughs in Maine. "He told me that he had several books in his study which I never saw . . . and [that] he could raise the devil."

Lewis described a vivid scene: the minister's study, which she knew so well; the sober leather volumes filled with sacred words; and behind them, another book—a black book, inscribed with vile spells and names written in blood.

When the Burroughs spirit was not trying to force Mercy to sign the book, he enticed her with evil images that were distortions of the most familiar passages in the Bible. He "carried me [to] an exceeding high mountain and showed me all the kingdoms of the earth and told me that he could give them all to me" if she joined his band of witches.

Burroughs did more than torture and tempt. He also held services for his evil band. Abigail Hobbs saw him convene a "general meeting of the witches in the field near Mr. Parris's house." Mary Warren knew how the witches gathered, for she saw Burroughs sound a trumpet to bring his hellish clan to a feast. Christians are accustomed to taking the Holy Sacrament as the Body and Blood of Jesus. Mary saw the satanic version of this: The wine the witches drank was real blood.

Holding in their custody the man who might well have brought the evil of witchcraft to Salem, Hathorne and Corwin brought in two other judges to help in their examination of Burroughs. They treated him as more than a mere witch. With the help of Judge Stoughton and Samuel Sewall, they cautiously questioned the prisoner alone before bringing him into open court.

The minister did not help himself. He declared with no hesitation that he had baptized only one of his seven children. This was, at the least, odd for a minister. It suggested that he might be a Baptist who did not believe in infant baptism—which extreme Puritans would see as a possible sign of being in league with the devil—or that he might simply be a devil worshiper outright. There are no records of the trial itself, though Cotton Mather's summary of the evidence given there sounds very much like the transcripts of Burroughs's pretrial hearings, which we do have. The accusers claimed Burroughs was no mere witch, but was of a higher order of evil. One said he called himself a "conjurer above the ordinary rank of witches."

By this point in the Salem episode some people had begun to confess that they actually were witches, and they now joined the parade of accusers. Burroughs seduced some with promises of nice clothes, they said, others with puppets and pins they could use to hurt their neighbors. As befitted such a dignitary of Satan, the behavior of the accusers went to new extremes. The judges could barely hear amid the din—not that there was much worth hearing, since many were so tormented that they were "incapable of speaking."

Burroughs tried to save himself by challenging the assumptions of the trials. He forcefully denied that a devil could use one person to torment another at a distance. Reading, or summarizing, an English book written thirty years earlier, he brought the voice of the skeptic directly into the heart of witch-plagued Salem. No matter what deals the devil might make, he quoted, "the grand error of these latter ages is ascribing power to witches, and by foolish imagination of men's brains . . . wrongful killing of innocents under the name of witches." If you were inclined to see Burroughs as an archvillain, this argument was like that of a murderer with blood on his hands playing dumb about his crime. If you agreed that the entire premise of the trials was wrong, Burroughs sounded remarkably clear-sighted and brave.

Burroughs must have known that his defense could not work, and as his execution date of August 19 approached, he made his peace with his life and his fate. On the day before he was about to die, he received a visitor in his cell. Margaret Jacobs, one of the confessed witches who had testified against him, came to beg forgiveness. Margaret admitted to him that she had lied. She had lied to help convict Burroughs, lied to help convict her own grandfather, George Jacobs, lied in her own admission of being a witch. According to Robert Calef's account, a nearly saintly Burroughs "prayed with her and for her." Just as the Salem pack was bringing down its biggest quarry, its forces were starting to crack.

Two different George Burroughses came to be hanged the next day—at least that is the impression left by the surviving records. According to Cotton Mather's account, during the trial Burroughs fought, lied, and denied, and, as a result, he was executed. Mather spent no time describing the hanging itself, for his sole point was that a very evil man, perhaps the human who worked most closely with the devil in creating the siege of witch-craft in Massachusetts, had been defeated. According to two critics of the trials, Thomas Brattle and Robert Calef, the execution scene itself was remarkable. There may have been an evil man in the guise of a minister there, but it was not Burroughs, who was the closest thing to a Christian martyr.

Calef described Burroughs passing through the streets of Salem in a cart before reaching the gallows.

There, Calef reports, Burroughs spoke in such a serious, solemn way about his own innocence that the
crowd began to listen to him. He prayed eloquently,
perhaps forgiving his accusers, and ended by sailing
through that old test of Cotton Mather's: a perfect
recital of the Lord's Prayer. He may have even asked an
attending minister to pray with him. By now the
crowd, gathered to see five witches killed, was in tears.
Samuel Sewall wrote in his diary that Burroughs's
"speech, prayer, protestations of innocence, did much
move unthinking persons." The crowd may even have
begun to turn, threatening to stop his hanging.

Cotton Mather himself may have been the minister Burroughs turned to in prayer—and the man who
sent him to his death. "Mr. Cotton Mather, being
mounted on a horse," Calef says, "addressed himself
to the people." Mather quieted the crowd, reminding
them that the devil could take the shape of even an
angel. If Calef's account is true, then Mather personally ensured that Burroughs would die and that the
trials would continue. Though historians are still at
odds over whether Mather was even present at
Burroughs's execution, it is possible that two men in
black faced off on Gallows Hill: one about to die, the
other rising to become the spiritual leader of his
colony; one speaking for himself, the other for the
rule of the group, the will of the majority; each one
seeing the other as a devil in the garb of an angel, but
which was which?

Few scholars today believe Burroughs was the arch-fiend Mather described. But that is not the end of the story. There is reason to believe, from the testimony against him, that he was the kind of wife-beating bully who seals off his family from contact with the outside world, abusing and intimidating them all into silence. The Putnams claimed that when Burroughs and his first wife lived with them, he enforced a pact of silence that forbade her from talking about their life. A neighbor from Casco Bay said that Burroughs's wife pleaded with her to write to her father, for her husband allowed her no contact with her family. If the Putnams were translating their family dramas into accusations of witchcraft, they may also have been using that same story to tell town secrets. Ann Jr.'s visions of the avenging wives could have been her way of revealing a horrible truth she had heard from her parents. So Mather could have been right in saying that Burroughs kept each of his wives in a "strange kind of slavery."

The possible dark side to George Burroughs opens up a larger question. Mercy Lewis's story of the devilish book in the minister's study, the outbreak of afflictions in the home of the Reverend Parris, and the many examples of accusers describing the devil in words very similar to those they had heard about God from ministers could be important clues. If the religious leaders of Salem had their own secrets, whether of wife beating or any other form of abuse, perhaps the young people of the town began to have nightmares about good and evil switching places, about men in black who spoke as gods in the service of devils. In the face-off of the two men in black, perhaps Mather spoke with the voice not only of the majority on a witch-hunt, but of a town angry at a man of God who betrayed his principles and was a tyrant to his own family.

That anger could also have had a completely different, though all the more potent, source. It is possible that it was Mercy Lewis who passed on some of the stories about Burroughs to the Putnams. At the age of three she had lived in Casco Bay, and she barely escaped with her parents and Burroughs when the Wabanaki attacked. In those raids her maternal grandparents and two of her uncles by marriage were killed and two aunts captured. Though Burroughs lived in a number of areas that suffered devastating raids, he apparently had an almost miraculous ability to survive. *Miraculous* could also imply either *devilish* or *traitorous.* Mercy—like Abigail Hobbs, who lived near her and Burroughs in Falmouth and then testified against him—could easily have believed that he had allied himself with the very Indians who had destroyed so many members of her family. There is no reason to think that Burroughs actually was in league with people who killed his neighbors, but as Mary Beth Norton has shown, there is every reason to assume that his accusers believed it of him.

CHAPTER VIII

"Choosing Death with a Quiet Conscience"

s for our So[vereig]n Lord and Lady the K[ing]
That Sarah Bucklby Wife of Willia[m]
In the County of Essex Shoom[aker]
[th]e Eighteenth day of May —
aforesaid and divers other days and
as after [C]ertaine detestable Arts
[call]ed Witchcraft Maliciously and fel[oniously]
[used] and Exercised At and in the Tow[n]
[Coun]ty of Essex — aforesaid in u[pon]
[Pu]ttman of Salem —
— by whic[h]
[Joh]n Puttnam y[e] Day & Yeare afor[esaid]
[and] times both before and after w[as]
[aff]licted Consumed Pined Wasted & [tormented]
[su]ndry other Acts of Witchcraft by
[Buck]lby — Committed and done before [and]
[again]st Our So[vereig]n Lord and Lady the
[Cr]owne & Dignity and the forme

"If I would CONFESS, I should have my LIFE"

The confession Margaret Jacobs made to George Burroughs, in which she admitted lying about being a witch, marks a turning point in the trials, for she undermined the implicit compact that had come to govern the accusations and hearings. Since late April more and more accused witches had taken the bargain Judge Hathorne had offered to Rebecca Nurse: Confess and be saved. When fourteen-year-old Abigail Hobbs was examined on April 19, she immediately said, "I will speak the truth. . . . I have been very wicked. I hope I shall be better, if God will help me." Like Tituba, she was cooperative, penitent, and willing to add details about the devil she had been meeting for three or four years. There were no fits among the accusers while Abigail spoke—there was no need for them. For instead of battling against her accusers, she used her examination to confirm their stories. It was as if Hobbs was signaling that she wanted to join the accusing band. Three of the leading accusers—Mercy Lewis, Abigail Williams, and Ann Putnam Jr.—immediately recognized the message and told the court they felt sorry for her.

Mary Warren, who worked for the Proctors, tried a variety of strategies when she came under suspicion. At first she claimed that the accusers were faking their afflictions. The judges could have seized the opportunity provided by this challenge to closely examine the claims of the accusers, but none of them did. And when the accusers started to howl during Mary's testimony, she went into her own fits. That form of creating a bond with her accusers did not win the sympathy of the accusers or the judges. Finally, while in prison, she began to confess. This strategy worked much better, for when she returned to her hearing, the accusers were silent as long as her story supported theirs.

Sarah Churchill and Margaret Jacobs, two other women accused of witchcraft, must have figured out the new rules. They did not deny the accusations against them. Instead, they offered confessions of their own.

By May anyone who was accused of witchcraft had a clear path to at least temporary safety. All he or she had to do was to confess to being a witch, confirm and elaborate the current story of the devil, his book, and his evil meetings, and name other witches—even if those named were already in jail or executed. Though a confessor would go to jail, only five were brought to trial at the court of Oyer and Terminer, and though they were convicted, none were executed. While those who resisted the court were being hustled to Gallows Hill at a faster and faster pace, those who confessed essentially joined the winning side and were often embraced by the accusers. It seemed that if you played the game the way they wanted you to, you were safe.

This system could have gone on without end, for as more and more people confessed, there seemed to be ever more proof of the need for the trials to go on. In July two unnamed accusers (often presumed to be young Ann Putnam and Mary Walcott, though Mary Beth Norton suggests that Mercy Lewis and Betty Hubbard are more likely candidates) were invited to go to Andover to search out witchcraft there. Soon growing numbers of Andover suspects were being called in for their hearings and trials. A new set of confessions kept expanding the size and nature of the witchcraft conspiracy.

There was only one problem with this self-perpetuating machine: To confess was to lie. And some of the confessors could not bear to have such horrible, deadly lies on their consciences.

Sarah Churchill was the first confessor to break

down. She said all the expected things about signing the book and using pins and puppets, and she confirmed the accusations against other obvious suspects, such as Bridget Bishop. By specifically admitting that she had harmed three of the leading accusers, including Ann Putnam Jr., Sarah clearly signaled that she wanted their forgiveness, which made her as safe as a confessor could be. But she was not safe from her own mind.

Though her confession was perfect, it was also perfectly false. Sarah believed the teachings of her faith. By lying, she had "undone herself." Now, agonized and in tears, she turned to Sarah Ingersoll—who was neither accused nor an accuser—and truly confessed. She admitted that she had never signed the devil's book. Ingersoll did not believe her retraction, but Churchill was adamant. "No, no, no; I never, I never did," she protested with all her heart. As she paced back and forth, despising herself for lying, she explained why she had made up her story. It was the only thing that would please one of the ministers, Reverend Noyes. "If she told Mr. Noyes but once [that] she had set her hand to the book, he would leave her [alone]; but if she told the truth and said she had not set her hand to the book, a hundred times he would not believe her." Not only did the ministers demand the story they wanted, they threatened to put her in a cell with the arch-villain George Burroughs if she recanted her confession.

Churchill's account did more than undermine the

growing testimony of the confessors. It also exposed the coercion taking place outside the hearings and trials. While the accusers showed signs of cooperation and a possible agreed-upon agenda in their fits, bites, and wounds, it seems that the judges and ministers now also had so much at stake in the cases that they could not allow any weakness in the stories. As Judge Stoughton set out in his charge to the jury, the overall case was too horrible to allow slips in the details to matter. Now some were making sure there were no slips. And yet Sarah Ingersoll loyally recorded Sarah Churchill's confession and preserved it for history. The fragile, hesitant voice of the individual struggling with her conscience began to be heard amid the crushing noise and orchestrated pageantry of the trials.

Margaret Jacobs did not just confess to the condemned George Burroughs. From the very moment that she went along with the accusers, she had been unable to sleep, knowing she had done wrong. "I was in such horror of conscience that I could not sleep for fear the devil should carry me away for telling such horrid lies," she said. She spoke directly to the judges and took back her testimony. She then set down her recantation on paper. It tells us exactly how an innocent person could be led to lie and to tell more lies even at the cost of condemning members of her own family to death. When Margaret came to court for her examination by the judges, she tells us, she was terrified by the displays of the accusers. She was overwhelmed, not knowing why they were so disturbed, but they insisted that she was harming them, and "if I would not confess, I should be put down into the dungeon and would be hanged; but if I would confess, I should have my life."

The tactics seem obvious to us now. First, a kind of psychological shock theater—a whole room of screaming, fainting people tells you that you and you alone are responsible for their suffering. Then a bargain offered—confess and be saved, fight us and be killed. Margaret went along and confessed, "which confession, may it please the honored court," she later admitted, "is altogether false and untrue." Her story had helped to condemn her own grandfather, as well as George Burroughs, to death, and she understood clearly what that meant for the state of her soul: "I saw nothing but death before me." Margaret was now willing to risk everything to undo what she had done. She chose "rather death with a quiet conscience than to live in such horror." Once she made her decision, though she was in a most horrible jail, "I have enjoyed more felicity in spirit, a thousand times, than I did before."

Sarah Churchill and Margaret Jacobs staked their lives against their consciences. Anyone who reads either woman's words can recognize the voice of a good person standing up against an oppressive machine. Sarah's and Margaret's words reached only a few people at the time, but the trials were open to the pub-

lic, and the power of truth in the mouth of a courageous person threatened to quiet the frenzy of the
accusers and to negate the arm-twisting of the court.

A CONFUSED
jury
Rebecca Nurse was a real challenge
for the court of Oyer and Terminer. Because the court
wavered, her case is one scholars of Salem have turned
to again and again. So much so, that at one point she
was turned into a kind of saint.

Though the accusations against Rebecca, led by the
Putnams, were enough to arrest and indict her, she still
had to be convicted. She and her supporters, spear-
headed by her determined family, rallied to her defense.
A petition in support of her character drew support not
only from the Porter faction, but even from some within
the Putnam clan. This is one sign that no matter how
closely linked the accusers were, they were not carrying
out a large, carefully planned and policed conspiracy. It
also shows that the tensions between the Putnams and
the Porters, however powerful, were not enough to
wholly explain the witchcraft accusations.

While the court weighed the opinions of Rebecca's
neighbors, the accused made her own plea. As was
quite often the case, a physical search of her body for a
telltale witch's breast yielded contradictory results. A
ten-person panel at first confirmed that she had one.
Then, just a few hours later, the panel decided she did
not. Rebecca asked for a third and final test. This was

playing by the rules of the court, but there is no record that it complied.

In person, the sickly, devout, earnest woman must have been impressive. She reached the jury, who began to see her as her neighbors did, not as the accusers painted her. For a moment the jury was able to look beyond Stoughton's instructions and the whole weight and momentum of the cases to see an individual, a good woman. They found her innocent.

Neither the accusers nor the judges would accept this verdict. According to Robert Calef, the court erupted in fury: "Immediately all the accusers in the court, and suddenly after, all the afflicted out of court made a hideous outcry." If Rebecca was not guilty, the whole mechanism of accusation, confession, and trial was in danger. One judge objected to the verdict, another threatened to storm off the bench. Stoughton was not so brazen. He was ready to accept the decision, but he returned to the testimony. He found a small ambiguity in something Rebecca had said that could be interpreted to mean she had inadvertently admitted to being in the company of witches.

The jury, which by this time must have been hesitant to acquit Rebecca, agreed to review the matter. They asked Rebecca to explain herself, but she didn't. Later on, too late, she said that she was simply too distraught and too hard of hearing to understand the question that was put to her. Whether because jury members truly believed Rebecca was guilty or whether they were too frightened to go against the howling mob and the justices who were clearly guiding them, the jury changed its verdict.

On July 19 Rebecca Nurse was hanged as a witch.

"Till the BLOOD was ready to COME out of their NOSES"

By the end of July six witches had been hanged and one had died in prison. Five more were executed in August and eight in September. Clearly, keeping the cases moving mattered a great deal to influential people. But why? And how far were these people willing to go to obtain confessions and convictions?

The court of Oyer and Terminer that Governor Phips created was a kind of X ray of the colony-in-transition he came to govern. As Nathaniel Saltonstall's hasty departure from the trials and the June 15 statement drafted by the Mathers and other ministers showed, there was serious doubt in the colony about the very basis of the trials the court was holding. And yet there seemed no stronger and clearer need than to wrap up the cases, find the witches, and execute them. Stopping the cases in order to debate the evidence risked letting the most dangerous threat the colony had ever faced go unchecked. But allowing the cases to go on as they were risked violating the very morality that was the colony's reason for existing. This is precisely the issue that Americans are debating today about the civil rights of suspected and captured terrorists. Perhaps it was this atmosphere of crisis—in which the power of the law was racing ahead of an annoying, yet persistent, thread of skepticism—that caused the court to abandon all precedent and both seek confessions and at least temporarily protect confessors. That is what it did in public. Within the prisons, it may have gone further.

Four days after Rebecca Nurse was executed John Proctor sent a plea from his own prison cell to five of the leading ministers in Massachusetts. The confessions that were moving the cases forward were being obtained, he claimed, by the most horrible means. For English Protestants, there was no institution more evil than the Spanish Inquisition. To them it represented the use of cruelty to suppress conscience. But, according to John, the judges were using the worst practice of those very Inquisitors right here in Massachusetts: torture.

John's own son was tied up in an obscene horseshoe, with his heels bound to his neck, until "the blood gushed out of his nose." He was supposed to stay that way for a full twenty-four hours, but a kindly jailer cut him loose. Two of the sons of the accused witch Martha Carrier were handled the same way, bound "neck and heels till the blood was ready to come out of their noses." Only this barbarous treatment convinced the children to turn against their parents.

Scholars believe that this nineteenth-century drawing shows the home of the Proctors. Arthur Miller used their stories as the centerpiece for his famous play *The Crucible*.

John's letter begged that the cases be moved to Boston, away from the obviously biased judges and their jailer henchmen. There is no record that the ministers responded to this plea. But even if they had, they were not in control of the colony. Their words were influential, but Governor Phips and the courts were not obligated to listen to them.

This letter and Tituba's accusation that Samuel Parris beat her are the only direct evidence we have of the use of physical torture in Salem. John may have been exaggerating or lying. It could be that an unusually cruel set of guards temporarily took the law into its own hands and that the ministers and judges responded to John's plea by attempting to make sure such abuse didn't happen again. But this one report of physical torture in the jail fits all too well with the atmosphere of psychological abuse that Sarah Churchill and Margaret Jacobs—and soon others—described.

The judges were leaders of a colony that was suffering defeats at the hands of the Wabanaki and the French. Their awareness that they could be blamed for these setbacks, as well as their belief that God was punishing the colony with both witchcraft and Indian attacks, could have been the inner motivation that drove them to believe the witchcraft accusations. But that is not the only possible reason for their behavior.

The majority of the judges were honorable men who thought they were doing their duty. Saving the colony as a whole from either actual witchcraft or the chaos caused by so many accusations may well have seemed more important to them than protecting a few suspects from being pressured into lying. It was even possible to read sixteenth-century English law as permitting torture in witchcraft trials, and it could be that the judges were following this precedent a century later in New England. Three of the judges, though, were linked to a scoundrel who found a way to turn the destruction of his neighbors to his own advantage.

Judge Corwin's house still stands in modern-day Salem, but this nineteenth-century drawing shows the home as it looked before it was renovated in the 1950s.

Only one building still stands in Salem that has a direct relationship to the trials. According to one theory, the home of Judge Jonathan Corwin should be seen as a memorial to greed. For it was Corwin's nephew, George Corwin, the sheriff of the county in which the trials were held, who turned the machine of accusation and confession into a private campaign of intimidation and theft. It is possible that Judge Corwin, Judge Wait Winthrop (another uncle of the sheriff's), and Judge Gedney (the sheriff's father-in-law) were at least aware of and perhaps part of Corwin's web of corruption.

The court of Oyer and Terminer added a second

kind of punishment for witches that went beyond execution. A convicted witch lost not only her life but her property, which was liable to be taken away and given to the king. In this way, the witch's family was punished as much as the witch herself, for it could lose everything it owned.

As the sheriff of Essex County, George Corwin enforced this part of the judgment. He did so with a vengeance. In some cases Corwin began his seizures while the accused were still alive. In others, according to his victims, he held property up for ransom by threatening to sell it off completely if he was not paid. He may have faked a story of a prisoner escaping (which would also allow the king to take the property) in order to extort a bribe from another family. What happened in the case of George Jacobs, Martha's grandfather, was typical. Corwin arrived at George Jacobs's house soon after he was hanged. Corwin and his men grabbed two feather beds with everything on them, all the furniture they could carry, five cows, and five pigs. He might even have attempted to take the widow Jacobs's wedding ring. Although in theory Corwin was simply collecting property for the king, he had ample opportunity to line his own pockets while doing so. And there is good evidence that in the case of the property of Philip English, where the most money was at stake, Corwin kept everything for himself.

While much about the Salem trials is subject to dispute, Corwin's trail of destruction is not. For as soon

as the families felt safe enough to do so, they went to
court to recover their property. It is less clear how
Corwin's actions were linked to what took place in
court during the witch trials. There could have been a
planned effort to steal, in which conspiring accusers,
corrupt judges, and cruel jailers worked with the
vicious sheriff. But Corwin's actions were erratic. He
did not consistently seek wealthy victims. We have no
record of what he took for himself and what he
reserved for the Crown. Nor did the accusers and the
court follow a clear pattern in the kinds of people
brought up on witchcraft charges. It is more likely that,
in an atmosphere of crisis, where fear and intimidation dominated, many individuals found ways to take
advantage of the events for themselves. For Judge
Stoughton, the main issue may have been stamping out
witchcraft, which could serve his long-range ambi-
tion to become governor of the colony. For Sheriff
Corwin, it may have been terrorizing his neighbors
and stealing their goods. All the other judges and jailers probably had their own mixture of motivations and
ideals, some torturing children by tying them up in
ropes and others risking their own safety by cutting
them loose.

When the skeptic Thomas Brattle challenged the
validity of the trials, he brought up one more accusation against the judges, and it had nothing to do with
torture or profit. He noticed that the court was completely inconsistent in dealing with accusations and the

treatment of the accused. When Judge Corwin's own mother-in-law was named, for example, she was never brought in for questioning. Though Brattle did not mention it, the court had dismissed out of hand an accusation against the prominent minister Samuel Willard. The court also failed to pursue a case against the wife of the Reverend John Hale, who was accused shortly after Brattle's letter was written. And while Philip and Mary English, Daniel Andrew, and John Alden were arrested, they easily escaped their light guard. The court made no consistent effort to bring them back, though the English family was living quite openly in New York.

Whether because of questions about the accusers and their dramatics, stories of torture and other illegal acts, or scandals about wealthy people seemingly above the law, by September there were more and more reasons for good people who believed in witchcraft to fear that something had gone wrong in Salem. Yet it still took great courage for individuals to speak up. Two of them did. And while it cost one her life, she remains in the eyes of history one of the true heroes of Salem.

CHAPTER IX

"That No More Innocent Blood Be Shed"

[...] the humble [...] [...] [...] [...]
Judge and Bench nowe sitting In Judicature in sale
and the Reverend ministers humbly sheweth

That whereas your poor and humble Petition being
demned to die Doe humbly begg of you to take it into your
dicious and pious considerations that your poor and hum
petitioner knowing my owne Innocencye Blised be the lord
it and seeing plainly the wiles and subtility of accusers by
selfe cann not but judg charitably of others that are
y same way of my selfe if the Lord steps not mightily in
confined a whole month upon the same
ccount that I am condemned now for and then cleared by the
afflicted persons as some of your honours knows and
cleared two dayes time I was cryed out upon by them
have been confined and now am condemned to die the lord
boue knows my Innocencye then and likewise does
that at the great day will be knowne to men and An
I Petition to your honours not for my own life foe
know I must die and my appointed time is sett but the
lord he knowes it is that if it be possible no more c
Lord blood may be shed which undoubtidly cannot be
Avoyde In the way and course you goe in I Question
but your honours does to the uttmost of your powe
in the discovery and detecting of witchcraft and witc
and would not be gulty of Innocent blood for the
world but by my own Innocencye I know you are
the wrong way the lord in his infinite mercye
you in this great work if it be his blessed will that
innocent blood be not shed I would humbly begg of you
your honours would be plesed to examine theis Afflicted
persons strictly and keepe them apart some time a
likewise to try some of these confesing witches I bein
confident there is seuerall of them has belyed themse
and others aswill appeare if not in this word I am su
in the world to come whither I am now going and I qu
on not youle see an alteration of thes things they say
selfe and others hauing made a League with the Diu
we cannot confesse I know and the lord knowes
will thorly appeare they belye me and so I Question
but they doe others the lord aboue who is the searche
all hearts knowes that as I shall answere it att the

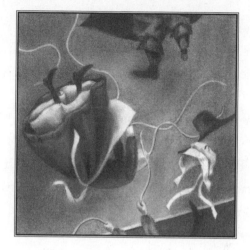

Mary
EASTY
Mary Easty came as close as any of the victims could to stopping the trials. Like Martha Corey and Easty's sisters Rebecca Nurse and Sarah Cloyce, Mary was very well thought of by her church and her community. Her pretrial testimony, taken in April, makes it easy to see why. As Judges Hathorne and Corwin pressed her with the usual questions, the power and sincerity of her words was striking:

JUDGE: How far have you complied with Satan?
MARY EASTY: Sir, I never complied but prayed

This is the first page (*left*) of the petition Mary Easty sent to the court of Oyer and Terminer. The phrase "no more innocent blood be shed" begins on the left half of the twenty-second line from the top.

against him all my days. . . . What would you have
me do?

JUDGE: Confess if you be guilty.

MARY EASTY: I will say it, if it was my last time, I
am clear of this sin.

JUDGE: Of what sin?

MARY EASTY: Of witchcraft.

Ann Putnam Jr., Mercy Lewis, Elizabeth Hubbard,
and Mary Walcott responded in their usual ways. When
Easty clenched her hands, Mercy seemed forced to
clasp hers, and Ann and Elizabeth interrupted to
scream, "Oh, Goody Easty, Goody Easty, you are the
woman, you are the woman."

Mary Easty must have been a powerful presence,
because this all-too-typical exchange had an unusual
result. By May 18 she was set free. She may have been
let off because the strong figure she cut in court was
backed up by her church. Mary's minister certainly
spoke up for her, and it is not unlikely that she
received other support. As in the case of Elizabeth
Proctor, when Deputy Governor Danforth challenged the accusers, it looked very much like Mary
could beat the charges without making a false confession.

But Mercy Lewis was adamant. By May 20 she was
in the most extreme fit of all, seemingly frozen for days
in a kind of rigid lockjaw from which death itself would
be a relief. The ferocity of Mercy's attack suggests a

kind of demented tantrum—as if she was furious that a woman she had accused might go free.

We are not certain why Mary was released. She later said that she had been "cleared by the afflicted persons," which suggests that, for one reason or another, some of the accusers had backed off. If that is so, Mercy's singular fit might have contained another message: rage that her allies were not rushing to join her in bringing Mary down. Perhaps Mercy was insisting, demanding in a way that only her allies would understand, that the game continue by the same rules: If one accuser named a suspect, all would confirm her story.

If Mercy was sending a signal to her sister accusers, they understood it perfectly. Ann Putnam Jr., Abigail Williams, and Mary Walcott all arrived at the house where Mercy was in her agonies, and all reported their own stories of seeing the attacking spirit of Mary Easty. With this new round of accusations against her, Mary was brought back for a second examination, probably on May 23. Based on that hearing, she was held for trial. The summer moved along with Mary in prison, not yet having to face the court. One trial date after another passed, suggesting that there was still some uncertainty among the judges about how to treat her. This gave her ample opportunity to observe firsthand how the cases were being run. Sometime in September, it seems, Mary and her sister Sarah Cloyce used what they had learned to petition the judges.

According to the legal procedures used at the time,

the accused had no right to representation in court and thus no informed sense of how to speak on their own behalf. But Mary was firm, clear, and fair. She and Sarah turned to the magistrates themselves, asking that "you who are our judges, would please to be of council to us." Then they used the power of their own deep and unmistakable faith to state their general position: They were not "conscious to ourselves of any guilt in the least degree of that crime whereof we are now accused (in the presence of the Living God we speak it, before whose awful tribunal we know we shall ere long appear) nor of any other scandalous evil, or miscarriage inconsistent with Christianity." In other words, they felt completely innocent, and this feeling, they wrote, was confirmed by "those who have had the longest and best knowledge of us." They had found neighbors and fellow church members, such as Mary's own minister, who were willing to testify under oath "what they know concerning each of us."

What stood, they asked, against the fervent and devout assertions of the accused and their reputations built over a lifetime? Simply "the testimony of witches, or such as are afflicted." With a logic that was almost mathematical, Mary Easty and Sarah Cloyce forced the judges back to the issue that Sarah Osborne and Rebecca Nurse and the ministers in their June 15 statement had all raised—the very issue that had hung over the events from the very beginning of the pretrial hearings, or even before, when the devil's own rye cake test pointed out the first suspect: How can you trust witches, or visions of their vile spirits, "without other legal evidence concurring"?

The joint petition was met with silence. In another sense, though, it spoke loudly. For it has remained in the record as an inescapable indictment of the Salem witchcraft proceedings. When even the sharpest logic could have no effect on the judges, Mary realized that her trial would be a formality and that she would soon die. Shortly before her execution date of September 22, she sent a second petition to the court. Here she rose from demonstrating her clear thinking to embodying a truly humbling saintliness. Like Dr. Martin Luther King Jr.'s final speech in Memphis the night before he was killed, it is the voice of the Bible brought into modern times.

"I petition to your honors not for my own life for I know I must die and my appointed time is set but . . . if it be possible no more innocent blood may be shed." Mary was speaking now almost from beyond the grave. With no hope of saving herself, she spoke simply as the conscience and soul of the community, grieving for everyone's suffering, even that of the judges. "I question not but your honors do to the utmost of your powers in the discovery and detecting of witchcraft and witches and would not be guilty of innocent blood for the world. But by my own innocence I know you are in the wrong way. The Lord in his infinite mercy direct you in this great work if it be his blessed will that no more innocent blood be shed."

Mary's plea to stop the killings repeated like a tolling bell, sounding through the clamor of the court, the racket of the accusers, the stress and strain of the judges' high mission: "that no more innocent blood be shed." One final time she looked at the actual cases and offered the judges a way out: "I would humbly beg of you that your honors would be pleased to examine the afflicted persons strictly and keep them apart some time." Here was a simple way to break the collusion of the pack and to test their claims: Examine them individually and see when and how their visions matched. Mary understood both sides of the machine of accusation and confession, and she ended by challenging the mechanism that kept the trials going. She suggested bringing the confessed witches to trial, "I being confident there is several of them have belied themselves." One final time she contrasted the easy lies of the confessors with the weight of her own conscience: "The Lord above who is the searcher of all hearts knows that I shall answer it at the tribunal seat that I know not the least thing of witchcraft therefore I cannot, I dare not, belie my own soul."

Sarah Churchill, Margaret Jacobs, and now, most powerfully, Mary Easty spoke for the individual heeding her own conscience against the pressure of the mob to conform and to lie. These heroes believed the teachings of their religion even as it seemed the leaders of their churches, courts, and the colony itself told them to play false and save themselves. We do not know who read Mary's petition or if perhaps an influential person might have helped her to write it. But it is clear that she and the others were finally heard.

"It was all FALSE"

On October 3 Increase Mather—arguably the religious and moral leader of Puritan Massachusetts—made the clearest possible statement on the trials. "The father of lies is never to be believed," he wrote. "He will utter twenty truths to make way for one lie. He will accuse twenty witches, if he can but thereby bring one innocent person into trouble." No matter how many spectral appearances there were, no matter how convincing and scary the fits, Increase argued, all of it was the devil's work and could not be trusted. Sounding like someone who had heard Mary Easty's call, Mather said, "To take away the life of anyone, merely because a specter or Devil, in a bewitched or possessed person does accuse them, will bring the guilt of innocent blood on the land." Finally and simply, he wrote, "It were better that ten suspected witches should escape, than that one innocent person should be condemned." With these words, and at the cost of perhaps twenty-five lives, the most active phase of the Salem witchcraft trials was over. Not one more witch was hanged.

The fearsome power of the accusers was broken. On October 8 Thomas Brattle sent a letter to an unknown person, which later became public. It cast a skeptic's cold and discerning eye on the cases. He objected strongly to Judge Stoughton for his zeal in prosecuting the highly

questionable cases and his impatience with any contradictory evidence. Brattle had been in touch with many
who shared his distaste for the trials, and he listed them
by name: from the honored ministers
Increase Mather and Samuel
Willard to the high government
officials Thomas Danforth
and Simon Bradstreet to
Judge Saltonstall and
"some of the Boston jus-
tices" who were resolved to
give up their seats rather
than have to prosecute
these cases; he was sure that
the leaders of Massachusetts
stood against Stoughton and his
conduct in the trials.

Increase Mather, Cotton's father, was
one of the most influential men in
Massachusetts. When he spoke
against the trials, it probably did a
great deal to stop them.

According to the letters he
sent back to London, Governor
Phips departed to deal with military matters not long after he cre-
ated the court of Oyer and Terminer. In other words,
he was far away and did not know much about the
actual convictions. Historians now have good evidence
that he had not left the area and had approved of the
proceedings of the trials. By October, though, when it
was clear that sentiment had shifted, he told London
that he was newly back in Boston and found "many
persons in a strange ferment of dissatisfaction." "The

Devil," he now believed, "had taken upon him the name and shape of several persons who were doubtless innocent and to my certain knowledge of good reputation." Mary Easty's logic and martyrdom, as well as the finality of Increase Mather's judgments, had reached the highest office in the land.

"I have now forbidden," Phips wrote, "the committing of any more that shall be accused without unavoidable necessity, and those that have been committed I should shelter from any proceedings against them wherein there may be the least suspicion of any wrong to be done to the innocent." On October 29 Governor Phips dissolved the very court he had created.

Mary Easty had predicted in her final petition that if confessors were brought to trial, the judges would see "an alteration of these things they say." Jailed with or near the confessed witches, she must have known how flimsy their statements were and how troubled they were about their own testimony. Once Increase Mather took his stand against the trials, he went on to question the confessors in prison. The overwhelming majority took back their statements. "It was all false," one stated simply. As Phips explained in a letter, "a black cloud" had "threatened this province with destruction." A "delusion of the Devil did spread . . . its dismal effects."

It was as if a spell had been cast over Massachusetts that had made it impossible for people to see or at least to speak the most obvious truths. That veil of distortion was now gone.

To deal with the existing cases, Governor Phips set up a new five-man court with some familiar judges, including Stoughton and Sewall, but also the skeptic Thomas Danforth. It took the judges and a series of juries the rest of the year to acquit all but three of the accused. But Stoughton was determined to prosecute, and he signed death sentences for those three accused witches as well as five left over from the cases of the previous court. Phips personally stopped the executions, pending word from London. Apparently, the chief justice was furious and stormed off of the bench. At least that is what Phips, now eager to show he was not responsible for the whole affair, reported to England. When the trials began, Judge Saltonstall quit to protest a manner of trying cases he could not support. Now Judge Stoughton quit to protest the end of that system. By midsummer of 1693 final word came from London: The pardons were approved.

"I do most HEARTILY, FERVENTLY, and HUMBLY beseech PARDON"

The dismissal of spectral evidence, the recantation of the confessors, the closing of the court of Oyer and Terminer, and the final freeing of all the accused and confessed witches left one set of people out: the accusers and their supporters. The logic of individual and group now entirely reversed, for it was the accusers who would have to face their neighbors, their future, and their consciences with blood on their hands. All the pressure they had brought on others to confess and be saved now came to weigh on them.

In August 1693 the Reverend Parris indicated that the events of the previous year were plaguing him. He preached a sermon on the death of Jesus that focused on how difficult it is to see someone suffer, especially when "those wounds we see, and that streaming blood we behold, accuses *us* as the vile actors. . . . Our consciences tell us that we, our cruel hands, have made those wounds, and the bloody instruments by which our dearest friend was gored." Mary Easty and perhaps even George Burroughs died as Christian martyrs, he seemed to now feel, which made him either Judas, who betrayed Jesus, or Pontius Pilate, who sentenced him to die.

By the fall of 1694 Parris was ready to make explicit what he had begun to describe as a generalized gnawing of conscience. Taking the lead in condemning witches, and along with them the Salem Town business mentality, had made him a leader, an important man, the ministerial spokesman for the Putnam clan. Now his job and his future were in jeopardy, and he begged forgiveness of God and of his congregation "of all my mistakes and trespasses in so weighty a matter." The confession was hedged, since Parris still hoped to stay on as minister in Salem Village. He stressed his effort to do the right thing. He appealed to the townsfolk for them to believe that he had been fooled by Satan, and he asked for mercy and kindness from his congregation. Parris's plea did not work. By the end of 1696, after many legal wrangles between his supporters and enemies, he resigned his post. Still, he broke new ground for all the judges and accusers by directly discussing his role in what was now clearly a grievous sin.

The Puritan leadership of Massachusetts took very seriously the covenant they had with God. In 1696, Samuel Willard, one of the ministers named by Thomas Brattle as an opponent of the trials, called the colony itself to account. If the trials were wrong, he argued, surely the faithful must ask God's pardon for having held and supported them. Both Cotton Mather and Samuel Sewall worked on drafts of a statement calling for a colony-wide day of fasting and prayer, which was to be held on January 14, 1697.

Sewall's draft was chosen to be used as a public statement, and it declared that recent setbacks in the colony, including a bad harvest, showed that "God is angry." And he ought to be, as they had made "mistakes" during the "late tragedy raised among us by Satan."

The declaration was no mere formality. It echoed the ministers' own inner thoughts. A year later Cotton Mather confided to his diary his fear that God would punish his own family "for my not appearing with *vigor* enough to stop the proceedings of the judges." Sewall's crisis of conscience took place in public.

On the day of penitence the Reverend Willard was to speak at Boston's South Church. Sewall's two-year-old daughter had recently died, and as the minister passed by his pew, the former judge gave him a statement to read out loud. Sewall stood up for all to see as Willard spoke these words: "Samuel Sewall, sensible of the reiterated strokes by God upon himself and family, and being sensible that, as to the guilt contracted upon the opening of the late [C]ommission of Oyer and Terminer at Salem . . . desires to take the blame and shame of it, asking pardon of men, and especially desiring prayers that God . . . would pardon that sin and all other of his sins."

The death of his daughter, Sewall believed, was the price he paid for his part in sending innocent people to die. If Parris waffled to try to save his job and Mather stated his most extreme self-blame where only God could see it, Sewall hid nothing. The Puritan conscience that would not allow Churchill, Cloyce, or Easty to lie forced Sewall to make his most private pain public knowledge.

A minister, a judge, and the colony as a whole had repented for their roles in the trials. Who was left? Twelve people who served on juries that meted out sentences in the witchcraft cases issued their own collective apology. They had been unable to make sense of the events at the time, they explained. Their apology was directed at the neighbors with whom they still lived: "We do therefore hereby signify to all in general (and to the surviving sufferers in especial) our deep sense of, and sorrow for, our errors."

There was still one disturbing and ominous silence: The accusers had not yet uttered a word.

CHAPTER X

"A Great Delusion of Satan"

...s for our Sou Lord and Lady the K...

That Sarah Buckly Wife of Willia...

In the County of Essex shoom...

he Eighteenth day of May — —

aforssaid and divers other days an...

as after Certaine detestable Arts

...ones Wickedly Maliciously and fele...

...d and Exercised At and in the Tow...

...ty of Essex — — Aforssaid in...

...ttman of Salem —

an — — — — — by whic...

...hn Puttnam y Day & Yeard Afor...

...and times both before and after 10...

...licted Consumed Pined Wasted...

...ndry other acts of Witchcraft by...

...kdy — Committed and done before...

...st Our Sou Lord and Lady the...

...rowne & Dignity and the forme...

Ann PUTNAM jr.

speaks   In 1697, Joseph Green, a young new minister, came to Salem Village. A wise and thoughtful peacemaker, he set out to heal his afflicted parish. Green rearranged the seating in his church, placing Ann Putnam Jr.'s father, Thomas, next to Samuel, the son of Rebecca Nurse, and Ann Putnam Sr. next to Samuel's wife. Rebecca's daughter was placed next to the mother of the accuser Mary Walcott. Day by day, service by service, neighbors would hear messages of understanding, charity, and forgiveness, and they would have the chance to put these fine words into practice with the person sitting right next to them.

Having set a tone of reconciliation in the church, Green urged the congregation to face the past by discussing the case of the executed Martha Corey, who had been excommunicated when she was convicted of being a witch. Green led the church to reverse that judgment.

Thomas and Ann Putnam Sr. both died in 1699, spent, perhaps, from the exhausting decade. They had fought back from reverses at the hands of the Porters and had risen to lead the colony in its most dramatic struggle only to end up seated penitently next to the local victims of their wrath. The deaths of her parents left Ann Jr., now nineteen, as the head of a large family of at least eight young children. Her afflictions that had seemed to flare up so dramatically in court, then disappear completely the next moment, now came home to roost.

Ann became chronically ill. One can imagine Ann in her twenties, worn down by fatigue, responsibility, and the weight of the past, starting to resemble the creature of fiction she claimed to have so often seen: the stooped and bitter hag. But Ann was an intelligent woman who understood that there was only one way toward a better life. She asked the Reverend Green to help her make peace with her neighbors.

Ann and her minister worked on a statement that he could read to the congregation, and he presented it to Samuel Nurse for approval. On August 25, 1706, Ann Putnam stood to face her neighbors while Green spoke. Ann admitted that as a child she had been an "instrument for the accusing of several persons of a grievous crime, whereby their lives were taken away from them, whom now I have just grounds and good reason to believe they were innocent persons."

The word *instrument* suggests that someone else was pulling the strings, but who? Ann's answer says little. "It was a great delusion of Satan that deceived me in that sad time." But what were her personal motivations? Again, she gives the same kind of vague and evasive answer. "I did it not out of any anger, malice, or ill-will to any person . . . but what I did was ignorantly, being deluded by Satan." Even in apologizing, Ann completely avoided responsibility. During the trials she claimed her injuries were inflicted on her by evil witches; now she blamed Satan for causing her to makes those false claims. Ann herself was strangely absent from her own self description.

Realizing, perhaps, that her neighbors could not accept such a general confession that said nothing about her specific role in the trials, Ann added, "I justly fear I have been instrumental, with others though ignorantly and unwittingly, to bring upon myself and this land the guilt of innocent blood." Mary Easty's words finally reached even her accuser.

Mary Easty, Rebecca Nurse, and Sarah Cloyce had clearly suffered great injustice, and Ann had to face her role in hurting them. "I was a chief instrument of accusing Goodwife Nurse and her two sisters," she admitted. "I desire to lie in the dust, and to be humbled for it, in that I was a cause, with others, of so sad a calamity to them and their families; for which cause I . . . earnestly beg forgiveness of God, and from all those unto whom I have given just cause of sorrow and offense, whose relations were taken away or accused."

Ann's confession reads like what it was: a compromise that was acceptable to her, speaking for the Putnams, and Samuel Nurse, as the representative of the accused innocents. It is more like a statement worked out by lawyers and public relations consultants than an expression of personal remorse. Nonetheless, the words she chose are revealing. Ann was the instrument, perhaps of others. Ann was a chief instrument, perhaps leading others. Ann was a victim, deluded by Satan. What do each of these phrases tell us?

If Ann was the tool of a conspiracy, it must have been one organized by her extended family. Detectives often try to crack a case by asking who benefited from the crime. That person is then a likely suspect. If the Putnams were engaged in a conspiracy, what was their aim? It is possible that Sheriff Corwin, working with his uncles, the judges, was the attacking arm of a cabal while Ann was the performing puppet. She ensured that the victims were tried and convicted, while Corwin collected their property. Thomas Putnam wrote a note to Judges Hathorne and Corwin that has an odd ring about it. Its tone is so grateful and fawning that it could be seen as referring to some other agreement between them.

"After most humble and hearty thanks presented to your honors for the great care and pains you have already taken for us," it begins, "for which we are never able to make you recompense (and we believe you do not expect it of us; therefore a full reward will be given you of the Lord God of Israel, whose cause and interest you have espoused, and we trust this shall add to your crown of glory in the day of Lord Jesus) . . ." It then goes on to hint at an astonishing new revelation to come.

The judges, Thomas is saying, have "taken great pains" for them—for the Putnams, not for God, not for the good people of Salem. Then, after mentioning the word *recompense,* he bends over backward to show that there is no money, no payoff, no "reward" involved except from God.

At the end of the note Thomas says he prays that the judges will continue to be "a terror to evil-doers and a praise to them that do well." Hathorne had used the very same aggressive phrase in his examination of Martha Corey, which suggests that Thomas was not just writing to the judge to give him information, but that he was also trying to impress Hathorne by showing him how well he had listened to the judge's words. That could be a kind of hidden nod: *You, judge, keep attacking, and thanks for supporting us.* This could be the only way Thomas could say in public, *Keep those cases moving, and we'll make sure the payoffs keep coming back to you.*

Thomas Putnam's note is suggestive but inconclusive, for the "astonishing new revelation" it was pointing to

was that George Burroughs was an evil, satanic man.
Though the Burroughs case was dramatic, it is difficult
to see any direct gain for the Putnams from his arrest
and execution. Thomas may well have wanted to make
sure of his alliance with the judges before his family
went after a man of the cloth. His angling for "praise"
does suggest a nod of mutual approval between the
judges and the accusers. If the Putnams were driven to
accuse Burroughs by secrets about his wives that the
family either knew they wanted to expose or that they
were just feeling as a growing compulsion expressed in
dreams and visions, that, too, could have made them
eager for support from the judges.

If the Putnams were engaged in a conspiracy aimed
at pure profit, they did it poorly, because they had little
to gain from their actions. The arrests and seizures of
land and property were too haphazard. There is no evidence that anyone in the family benefited financially
from the trials. And they spent a great deal of time and
effort on accusations—that of George Burroughs, for
example—that had nothing to do with property at all.
It is possible that their aim was merely to terrorize neighbors they envied, did not like, or with whom they had
long-standing conflicts. But that kind of rage seems less
like a coolly calculated strategy than a series of unplanned
steps in which each new arrest, trial, or conviction
sparked new accusations. It was the result not of planning, but of urges the actors themselves did not
completely understand.

Ann may have been the instrument of a family drama—the story of the evil stepmother who was stealing the Putnams' inheritance—that was transformed into a colony-wide witch-hunt. But there is no evidence she was the tool of a family plot.

The only other sense in which Ann might have described herself as an "instrument" would be if, as Mary Beth Norton argues, Mercy Lewis was the real leader of the group of accusers and Ann took actual or implied directions from her. That is a possible interpretation of her words, and it would give us an entirely new image of Ann—as a pawn whom another strong-willed girl was able to dominate. It will be an interesting challenge for future historians to see if viewing her this way yields new insights into the trials.

The accusers were remarkably coordinated in their actions, and this orchestration improved as the hearings and trials went on. The accusers' ability to turn on fits at the sight of the supposed witches, only to top them the instant an alleged witch began to apologize or confess, and the incredible ease with which they produced props in court all suggest some degree of control and planning. If they did consciously rehearse, plot, and calculate their performances, it is possible that Ann was "the chief instrument," at least among her peers. What did the accusers—not the clan, but the actors in court—gain from their deadly theatrics? Here, conscious and unconscious drives blur. The satisfactions to the accusers may have been subjective and emotional. What began as "sport," even the wicked game of getting to be "bad" in public and causing grief for adults, soon may have had other pleasures: being a star, being in control of others' fates, having power, harming those you disliked, and all the while being approved by your parents, your minister, the grandest, most important men in the land. Perhaps the accusers met to plan, or maybe they just got better and better at reading one another's signals. They may not have clearly known what they were going to do next and still have gotten great pleasure out of doing it.

From a modern point of view, the "delusion of Satan" could have been an ever-growing emotional momentum in which doubts that any single person had were trumped by both the excitement of what was happening and the impossibility of turning back. The only thing that could break the nightmarish pact that the participants made without even consciously knowing they had done so were the voices of people who refused to go along with their game. In a famous children's tale it took one child to notice that the emperor had no clothes. In the Salem witch trials it took a series of courageous individuals listening to their consciences and overcoming their fears to show that their town had no witches.

To the distinguished Salem scholar Bernard Rosenthal, though, all this talk of unconscious pacts and emotional drives is unnecessary. He argues that Ann and the other accusers knew that they were making up their fits and were completely aware that their lies were killing people and destroying lives. They may have tasted evil and liked it.

These conflicting views on the accusers' ultimate motivations form the most compelling mystery of the Salem witch trials. Every reader who studies the court records and accounts of the time will have to judge this for him- or herself. The story of Salem demands that we try to understand exactly where responsibility ended and compulsion began. Across the centuries this has been a difficult and fascinating challenge that the incomplete evidence has left to each of us.

Finally, and most speculatively, Ann's use of the word *instrument* suggests one other possible way of looking at the Salem story. In the 1950s and '60s young people in the United States and Europe started to listen to, buy, and play rock'n'roll. To them, and to their parents, the new music's sexuality, loudness, and "attitude" seemed the opposite of the smooth ballads and carefully produced show tunes that were mainstream favorites. Many adults who were pleased with their safe suburban lifestyles condemned rock as "primitive," while young people thought it was honest and exposed the hypocrisy underlying their parents' false image of "happiness." At the time there seemed to be an absolute divide, or generation gap, between the groups, with music as the battle line. This sense of divide was especially acute by the late '60s, when the young began to hold angry, sometimes violent, often provocative street protests and staged plays, filmed movies, and thrilled to music that celebrated this mood of rebellion. More recently, though, historians have looked back on that rebellious generation and have noted continuities between the music and "truth" they supported and the homes in which they had grown up.

Ann grew up in a Salem that was supposed to be a city of peace, united in a solemn covenant that bonded neighbors to one another and to God. But the Salem she knew was filled with disputation, argument, and malice. Reading through the endless accusations in the trial records, one sees decades of animosity that had festered in the town. There was not only the split between the Porters and the Putnams. Petty hostilities raged between neighbors over livestock, land, and the tensions of daily life. When Ann and others began to interrupt services and to take over hearings, they could be seen as creating a kind of unconscious protest. Without quite knowing it, they were saying that the reality of their town was not peace, not piety, not sharing. It was screeching, yelling, accusing. The young people were disrupting a pretense of peace and replacing it with a mirror of the true petty warfare and hypocrisy they experienced daily.

Though they were certainly not conscious of this, either, they may even have gone a step further. In the church, as the founders of Salem saw it, the "relation" was a wonderful moment. As a person told the whole community of experiencing God's grace, everyone was confirmed in his or her own faith and in the hope that theirs was a purified congregation of true saints. The machine of confession-and-acceptance that took shape in the court of Oyer and Terminer was a sort of reverse image of the relation. A person confessed her sins and was welcomed into the community. These sins did not point to God and his grace—though some of the stories of the devil made him sound like God. Instead, they showed how a person had fallen in league with a false god. Only confession of this sin could lead to forgiveness from the accusers. The admitted witches joined with the afflicted accusers in a new community. Without even knowing it, the accusers may have felt a kind of security in a familiar religious ritual, now in a new form.

Like the young people of the 1960s, the accusers found truth in yelling, screaming, and disrupting and in rituals that tried to bring new life to their parents' ideals by turning their ceremonies upside down. Subconsciously, too, they may have been attempting to show the real Salem to its citizens while trying to find a way past all that pettiness and anger to the place of confession and covenant inhabited by saints. The dark side of the 1960s came in the violence young rebels supported in the name of peace. Rejecting easy pieties made it all too tempting to them to embrace boundless aggression. Similarly, in Salem, the accusers may have held a mirror up to their parents and neighbors, but they also unflinchingly held up a hangman's noose. If Ann was an instrument of a kind of truth, it was a truth that came with a high price.

Wheels WITHIN
wheels
Thomas Putnam's note to the judges used one vivid phrase for the revelation he was about to share: "a wheel within a wheel." George Burroughs was actually the inner hub to which he was referring, but the image serves to characterize the entire Salem crisis.

Something caused a number of young people and a few of their elders in Salem Village to behave in strange ways that were reminiscent of the Goodwin children in Boston four years earlier. It may have been easier for them to blame a slave and other typical witch suspects than themselves for what was soon called their "affliction." The slave, in turn, was eloquent in shifting the focus of blame to a broader evil of which she herself was a victim. The local minister and his embattled supporters, who were falling behind their more successful competitors in another part of the town, were inclined to believe the slave's story. Peers and relatives of the initial accusers, perhaps driven by tensions in their own families, perhaps half knowing town secrets they felt compelled to reveal, perhaps simply seeing it all as "sport," joined in. Finally, young people who had seen family members murdered before their eyes and had heard rumors of betrayal in high places began to describe devilish attacks that resembled the physical ones they had experienced.

So the innermost wheel could have consisted of inbred local and family pressures, as well as wartime traumas, becoming a public crisis, while a slave accustomed to using language to protect herself with her masters became regarded as a truth-teller. In a colony beset by fierce attacks that its leaders seemed powerless to repel, it fell to local judges to make the initial response. They tried to be stern and efficient, though it is possible some also saw a way to make some illegal profit out of the uproar. The judges tended to believe accusers and distrust the accused, which encouraged further accusations.

In the second wheel words flung out in fits were turned into arrests, hearings, and imprisonments. Leaders of the colony grew alarmed and tried to guide and moderate the judges. But what began as a local problem now resonated with central concerns for the religious men who saw their people as having a special mission from God. The accusations seemed to confirm both the moral decline of the colony and the need for ever-greater vigilance. A new governor eager to court popularity in both England and New England established a court that could hand out death sentences, then took no public role in the crisis until the mood of the colony shifted.

Yet a third wheel turned a string of holding cells into a death row. There was no single cause for the fate of the accused witches. Rather, it was the alignment of forces—personal, local, and colony-wide—that was at fault. Once skeptics, martyrs, and ministers nudged the wheels apart, the machine stopped.

The Puritan ministers believed that witches were real and should be killed. After the Salem trials they could never again successfully act on that belief. But that is only a part of their legacy. Puritans believed in personal responsibility, the great moral weight of knowing you could never escape God's judgment. The moral courage of the accused who could not lie was also a reflection of their Puritanism.

The Puritans did not succeed in creating a colony according to their laws. William and Mary, the new English rulers, insisted that the Puritans must tolerate other faiths in their communities and give up legislating their rules through the government's courts. The Puritans' greatest success, though, came in teaching individuals to expect the most of themselves and not to compromise their standards at any cost. The crisis at Salem diminished Puritan leaders' control over their society as a whole, but it also showed that some people had taken Puritan teachings into their hearts and minds. Conscience proved to be stronger than even a society dedicated to enforcing the dictates of faith.

The horror inspired by hanging witches helped to ensure that Puritan laws, and ultimately the doctrines of any faith, would not set the rules by which all peoples in what was first British North America and later the United States would live. Govern-mental actions, courts, and sentences were not the way to bend people to any one interpretation of God's will. There was simply too much danger of using faith to destroy innocent people.

The core essence of Puritanism, though, did

endure in America. At its best it remained as a moral imperative, an unquenchable voice of conscience that those who opposed slavery and fought for women's rights and defended immigrants and exposed pollution have listened to ever since.

Explaining Salem

...rs for our Sov[erei]gn Lord and Lady the Kin[g]
...That Sarah Buckley Wife of Willia[m]

In the County of Essex Shoom[aker]
...he Eighteenth day of May —

...e aforesaid and divers other days an[d]
...as after Certaine detestable Arts
...corsed Wickedly Malitiously and fel[oniously]
...ed and Exercised At and in the Tow[ne]
...nty of Essex — Aforesaid in
...uttman of Salem
...an — — — by whi[ch]
...hn Puttnam y Day & Yeare afo[resaid]
...and times both before and after u
...flicted Consumed Pined Wasted C
...ndry other Acts of Witchcraft b[y]
...kby — Committed done before
...nst our Sov[erei]gn Lord and Lady the
...rowne & Dignity and the form

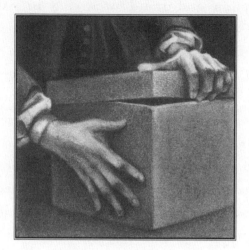

Fraud, witches, HYSTERICS,

hallucinators
Ever since the witch trials ended in the Massachusetts colony, people have tried to make sense of what happened. I have tried to outline the events, point to the best sources, and indicate some key questions that historians have raised. If you continue reading about Salem, you will soon discover that authors have strong opinions about what took place there. In order to help you make sense of those views, here is an outline of the different camps and how current scholars tend to view them. I discuss many of the most significant sources in greater detail in the "Notes and Comments" section as I cite them.

The oldest point of view is that there was some kind of deception and fraud occurring in Salem. The accusers made up their displays. Robert Calef and Thomas Brattle, who witnessed some of the events and gathered information from participants, saw the trials this way. Calef, in particular, also blamed Cotton Mather for supporting the accusers and defending the executions. In the nineteenth century Charles Upham collected many documents and local stories and followed that interpretation when he published his two-volume work *Salem Witchcraft*. He wrote well and had many wonderful details at his command, which made his work the foundation that both popular authors and serious historians used for over a century.

Two still-popular books can be seen as continuing this tradition of highly readable writing that tells a clear story of deception by the accusers and criticism of leading ministers, especially Cotton Mather: Marion Starkey's *The Devil in Massachusetts* and Arthur Miller's play *The Crucible*. Written in the late 1940s and early 1950s, respectively, these works depicted a clear clash between rigid, even murderous, religious thinkers and the dawning of a new and more rational modern temperament. Though authors at the time could read the original transcripts of the pretrial hearings, these were available only in their original form or as gathered, edited, and published by a team of scribes in the 1930s.

In 1969 Chadwick Hansen published *Witchcraft at Salem*. He thought all previous views, going back to

Upham's, were wrong. Hansen carefully reread the testimonies and decided that there truly were witches in Salem, which is one reason why the experiences of the accusers were real to them. He also began to sort through the mixture of evidence and legend that Upham and those who had followed him had blended together. For example, he showed how Tituba had changed in these accounts from an Indian to a black or half-black person over time.

A few years later Keith Thomas published a lengthy study, *Religion and the Decline of Magic*. Though his focus was England, Thomas opened new approaches to Salem for historians, for he examined in great detail the court records of accusations of witchcraft and other types of magical practice. He saw that various folk beliefs were quite common. Witchcraft accusations, he discovered, tended to cluster around certain people in a community, especially women who were perceived as angry outsiders; he also showed that definitions of magic changed over time. For example, astrology shifted back and forth from being acceptable to being seen as devilish to being viewed as simply ineffectual or wrong. Thomas argued that as communities much like Salem shifted from a view in which everyone was expected to look out for everyone else to a focus on each individual and family being out for itself, people felt guilty for not taking care of outsiders. In order not to have to feel badly, they then called those people witches.

Though historians have objected to parts of

Thomas's work, he offered a new way of seeing Salem. Folk magic and accusations of witchcraft were a part of English life. Instead of Salem as a horrible example of American Puritanism, it can be seen as the final expression of an interesting and complex strand in English history.

In the 1970s more and more historians began to study documents in America to see how witchcraft cases in the United States fit with those Thomas had described. At the same time two historians teaching an undergraduate course at the University of Massachusetts decided to take a new approach. Upham had indicated that there were deep tensions in Salem before the very first accusations of witchcraft. In *Salem Possessed,* Paul Boyer and Stephen Nissenbaum meticulously reconstructed those struggles. They defined in wonderful detail the feud between the Putnams and the Porters. Concise, well written, and full of fascinating insights, this book remains one of the glories of Salem studies. The witchcraft cases, it now seemed, had roots in traditional English practices and in local tensions. The two historians also published modern editions of the transcripts and of other relevant documents in their three-volume *Salem Witchcraft Papers*. They made it much easier for others to follow their trail and make sense of the events for themselves.

John Putnam Demos in *Entertaining Satan*, published in 1982, did not primarily focus on Salem, which is itself interesting. His concern was not to assign praise or assess blame to those involved in the trials, but to understand the larger picture in which those accusations fit. His richly researched and highly thoughtful book attempted to understand the psychology of witchcraft accusers. He made a serious effort to read through court testimony to understand the fears and anxieties inside people's minds.

In the 1980s historians, most notably Carol Karlsen in *The Devil in the Shape of a Woman*, took up the statistical information Thomas and others had found about women and witchcraft. If women were accused four times as often as men, this was significant. It told a great deal about how women in general were viewed in society. Karlsen in particular argued that the accused witches were not outsiders or bitter malcontents, but rather older women with some property. The conspiracy, in a sense, shifted away from the accusers in Salem. The real villain was a world that could not accept women who were not solely daughters, wives, or mothers.

The focus on the place of women in the whole issue of witchcraft continues to draw the attention of historians, though not mainly in regard to Salem. For in Salem, unlike any other similar outbreak of accusations in America, a significant percentage of men were accused and executed.

The three hundredth anniversary of the Salem trials in 1992 saw the publication of a book that challenged the shift in thinking that began with Hansen. The professor of English Bernard Rosenthal reread the original sources and went back to the older views. It was obvious, he argued in *Salem Story*, that there was conscious fraud in Salem. He also continued Hansen's effort to clear away the sludge of misinformation to which historians were still prey. His book is a refreshing, clean view that makes you read carefully and gives examples of collusion that seem unquestionable. Rosenthal is preparing his own new edition of the transcripts that corrects errors in the Boyer and Nissenbaum collection, rearranges the cases in a much more useful chronological sequence, and includes a smattering of documents that have recently been uncovered.

In the 1990s popular authors were inspired by Hansen in a different way. Combining his argument that there were real witches in Salem with other sources that claimed witchcraft was a part of an alternative female-oriented faith, they claimed the accused of Salem as long-lost ancestors. The issue of the witch trials was not fraud or true belief, they argued, but a society that could not accept a real pagan faith. An example of this kind of writing is Selma Williams's *Riding the Nightmare*, which was first published in 1978 and reprinted in 1991.

Academic historians have also followed up ideas from Hansen and Thomas and investigated how folk magic actually functioned in New England. Examining, for example, the diary of the judge Samuel Sewall, David Hall in his *Worlds of Wonder, Days of Judgment* found that a truly devout Puritan also harbored folk beliefs. So society was not split between harsh Puritan ministers trying to enforce their brand of Christianity and local people who may have outwardly conformed but secretly used magical practices. Instead, according to Hall, these beliefs mingled, even inside the minds of individuals. Folk practices influenced ministers, even as the religious leaders tried to stamp them out.

In the 1980s and '90s, Americans became more sensitive to the effects of child abuse, but several scandals in which children were led to give false testimony also exposed the danger of too easily accepting accusations of abuse. Recent books such as Peter Charles Hoffer's *The Salem Witchcraft Trials* have raised the possibility of using both of these insights to make sense of Salem: Perhaps there was a history of abuse in Salem; or can our more recent experience allow us to better understand the false claims of the past?

Today historians see both sides of Salem. The outbreak of accusations made use of long-established beliefs about folk magic, but it probably also included instances of conscious deceit or fraud. Our knowledge of the worldview of the accusers, the accused, and the rest of the people of Massachusetts at the time is much deeper than it was. But we still do not know for sure why people behaved as they did in Salem.

A number of medical researchers have tried to explain Salem in other ways. For instance, one theory posits that people in the town were eating bread made of spoiled wheat. The particular kind of rot, called *ergot*, in some wheat can have the effect of a drug that drives people temporarily mad, giving them visions and tormenting their bodies in ways similar to what the accusers described. Scientists and historians have looked closely at whether this could have taken place in Salem and have agreed that the theory is incorrect. Some of their reasons for coming to this conclusion are technical, having to do with climate, temperature, wheat crops, and the rise and fall of accusations in Salem. But there are also broader reasons for being hesitant about any such explanation of the trials.

The problem with this kind of approach can be easily seen in Laurie Winn Carlson's *A Fever in Salem*. She believes that those afflicted in Salem, and in general those who seemed to have been bewitched over the centuries, suffered from encephalitis lethargica, a disease whose symptoms match some of what was reported in Salem and that she believes could have been spread by birds and other animals. Her book is sloppy in places, but its biggest failing—which is also the flaw in the wheat rot theory—is that it assumes that you can look at symptoms and entirely disregard the cultural context in which they arose and were reported. While the references to such symptoms as biting, choking, and having visions come up over and over again in the trial records, it is hard to be sure what they really mean. The transcripts were not taken down by a stenographer or recorded on tape. The individuals writing them down could have developed a shorthand to summarize what they heard. The accusers might have done the same, or, as I have discussed, they might have been inventing their actions wholly or partially. We simply do not know what words like *pinching* actually described, which makes it impossible to treat them as medical clues.

It seems not only unlikely, but rather fruitless, to look for some single and simple biological explanation of witchcraft, which is as interesting for what it tells us about its time as for any "cause." But there is another possibility. It may be that over the centuries some people in England and New England did eat rotten wheat or suffer from exotic diseases and, as a result, had convulsions and visions. Doctors and ministers trying to heal them may have interpreted those symptoms as defining affliction, bewitchment, or possession. Then, when people in Salem began to think they were afflicted—or decided to fake being in that state they might have followed the known pattern of symptoms. A simple way this could have happened is if the Goodwin children in 1688 took some of their cues, consciously or unconsciously, from these established patterns and if the Salem accusers were then influenced by Cotton Mather's report on that case.

In other words, it was not germs that created symptoms that people falsely thought of as witchcraft; rather, when people believed they were afflicted, they behaved as they believed such people behaved, with a set of symptoms that might somewhere along the way have been observed in those suffering from one disease or another.

Most recently, there have been books, like this one, that seek to draw on and meld existing research. The best of these is Larry Gragg's *The Salem Witch Crisis*. A biographer of Samuel Parris, Gragg is quite familiar with both the original sources and the later studies, and he gives a readable, informed picture of what took place. Elaine G. Breslaw's *Tituba, Reluctant Witch of Salem* is an effort at a kind of biography of this crucial actor in the drama. It combines social history, detailed research, and speculation in trying to bring into focus the woman who was so important to the trials but who disappeared from history after they ended.

While researching this book, I learned of an important new study of Salem by the historian Mary Beth Norton. She generously informed me of an article she had published, "Finding the Devil in the Details of the Salem Witch Trials," which allowed me to get a sense of her ideas. Then, just as my book went into its final stages, I had the chance to read her *In the Devil's Snare*. Remarkably, Norton has managed to cast an entirely new light on the trials. By researching connections between a key group of accusers and severe clashes with Wabanaki people in Maine, she has supplied a context other historians only grasped in outline. This allowed her to make sense of accusations that had previously seemed random, to reinterpret pressures on the judges, and to take the accusers' visions seriously. Born out of her interest in women and girls as actors in their own right, this blend of a feminist orientation with a broad historical scope is certain to become a necessary book for the next generation of scholars. And in the future, as our own concerns make us look at the world in new ways, I am sure new schools of interpretation will arise. I know that the terrorist attacks of September 11, 2001, gave me a fresh sense of how differently one views the world in a time of crisis. As we examine our own ways of experiencing the world, we may well learn more about the accusers, judges, and victims of 1692.

THE CRUCIBLE, Witch-hunt, and Religion: Crossing Points of Many Histories

In classrooms throughout this land, Arthur Miller's play *The Crucible* is treated as a kind of direct view across the centuries into the hearts and minds of the Puritans and farmers of colonial New England. That is a mistake. And yet the play is a brilliant creation, well worth the attention it gets. The real question that should be preoccupying teachers and students is why *The Crucible* is such a compelling portrait of a witch-hunt if it does not draw its power from insight into the events of 1692. What is the truth that the play captures if it is not the specifics of the Salem trials? The answers to these questions make Miller's creation all the more relevant to young people now, in the wake of the September 11 attacks, than it would be if it were merely a cleverly written history lesson.

Having at his command in 1952 only a well-written but unreliable nineteenth-century local history, and the popular but inaccurate *The Devil in Massachusetts* by Marion Starkey, as well as the original pretrial transcripts, which themselves contain subtle errors that close readers have since corrected, Miller was wrong about some of his facts. He consciously combined characters, and the main lines

These sketches (*left*) for the original Broadway production of *The Crucible* show how the designers used space to tell a story. The small windows and dominating wooden beams are similar to the portholes and planks of a ship. The support beams also suggest a giant cross. Puritans would not allow images of the crucifixion in their home or churches, but, the setting and play suggest, in the name of Jesus they were carrying out their own persecution.

of his interpretations do not match the views of modern historians. To pick the most obvious example, in Miller's 1997 autobiography, *Timebends*, he recalls having "no doubt that Tituba, Reverend Parris's black Barbados slave, had been practicing witchcraft." As readers will have seen me mention in a number of places, since the early seventies when an English professor carefully reread the original sources, scholars have known that Tituba was Indian, not African, and that if she used any ritual or folk magic at all, she learned the practices from her English neighbors and owners. Anyone who would like to see a listing of all of the historical errors in Miller's play can go to Web sites such as http://ogram.org/17thc/miller.shtml, which has links to many Crucible sites, including ones that spell out historical inaccuracies in great detail.

Despite these "flaws," the "gotcha" satisfaction of pointing out places where the play does not match the historical record is a cheap and easy victory. It is a triumph of easy erudition that makes the critic the superior mind for seeing mistakes, without granting Miller his true achievement: his ability to make us believe he has it right.

The Crucible should be used in classrooms as a wonderful example of historical fiction, not because it is fiction that teaches us history, but because its very historical limitations show us the power of fiction to create a scene that feels real, vivid, and true. Accuracy to events does not make historical fiction ring true. The more you know about the history behind the Salem trials, the more you appreciate Miller's ability to

create characters who *ought* to have existed, even if they
didn't, stories that you *know* emotionally to be true,
even if they weren't. His confident and insightful sense
of psychology; his thoughtful, well-researched scene-
setting; and his deft characterization are all testimony
to his greatness as a writer, *not* his deep knowledge of
the past.

A writer has the ability to render something that
feels three-dimensional, that feels real. For some reason many people—from teachers, parents, and book
reviewers to talk show hosts associate this artistic ability,
this mastery of craft and technique, with a moral qual-
ity: a manner of truth-telling that is grounded in the
world outside of art. In other words, if you are good,
sincere, honest, and true, that will shine through in
your book. And if your historical novel is absolutely
faithful to fact, readers will experience it as a vivid portrait of the past. Like Hollywood costume designers who
used to make sure stars in movie biographies wore his-
torically accurate underwear, getting the hats, buttons,
and turns of phrase right in your work is seen as a sign
that you really care about the past, which will make your
novel "good."

The Crucible puts the lie to this view. It reminds us
that at least half of historical fiction, the "fiction" part,
is pure invention. Miller's play is good because he
makes the world he has invented come alive, not
because it captures life as it actually was lived.

The Crucible is, though, not simply a triumph of
artistry. As Miller so vividly explains in *Timebends*, he saw

an obvious link between the activities of a committee of
the House of Representatives, the House Un-American
Activities Committee (HUAC) and the trials as portrayed
in Starkey's book. HUAC was relentlessly pursuing tales
of a vast Communist conspiracy in America. At the time,
politicians, some motivated by sincere concern, others
taking advantage of the moment, made more and more
of a mood of suspicion that was sweeping the country.
HUAC began to hold hearings, questioning people about
whether they were or had ever been Communists. Large
businesses, schools, and media companies were put
under pressure to root out employees with dangerous
beliefs. People stood in danger of losing everything they
had built in their adult lives: careers, friendships, standing in the community. In an atmosphere of fear, some
protected themselves by speaking out against others.
Precisely as in Salem, the more people who confessed to
having been Communists and named others, the more
reason there was to hold hearings, bring in more suspects, and pressure more companies to purify their
ranks.

The Crucible, therefore, is a play about a witch-hunt in
the seventeenth century written to expose a witch-hunt
in the twentieth. And Miller hit upon an emotional
truth in his research. "The main point," he realized, "of
the hearings, precisely as in seventeenth-century Salem,
was that the accused make public confession, damns his
confederates as well as his Devil master, and guarantee
his sterling new allegiance by breaking disgusting old
vows—whereupon he was let loose to rejoin the society of

extremely decent people." Miller saw the witch trials as a kind of ritual cleansing, in which guilt could be released through confession and naming other sinners. That insight into the structure of the Salem hearings is true, or at least is true of a phase of them once accused witches began to confess. Probing into his own time, Miller understood the psychodynamics of the past, even if he did not entirely get the details right.

Miller had a subject that could speak to a current crisis while illuminating a fascinating historical moment, but how could he shape that into a play? He had an image in mind via the character he imagined for John Proctor: a good man who had once had an affair with a seventeen-year-old maid, and now had to face her leading a pack of accusers that was taking aim at his own wife. At that time Miller had entered psychoanalysis because he was haunted by the mutual attraction he and Marilyn Monroe had felt when they met briefly in Hollywood. Though he had not yet begun a relationship with Monroe, he felt that he was betraying his own marriage through his desire for Monroe. Procter might well have been a fictional depiction of Miller's dilemma, the emotional force of the play also emerged out of his own life.

As he was about to leave to go to Salem to read the pretrial transcripts, Miller received a call from the brilliant film director Elia Kazan. Miller knew, even as he drove to Kazan's Connecticut home, what he was about to hear. To save his career in Hollywood, Kazan had joined the modern-day witch-hunt. He had spoken to HUAC, and given them the names of people he claimed had once been Communists. Miller was not shocked, but he was angry. "It was not his [Kazan's] duty to be stronger than he was, the government had no right to require anyone to be stronger than it had been given him to be, the government was not in that line of work in America. I was experiencing a bitterness with the country that I had never even imagined before, a hatred of its stupidity and its throwing away of its freedom. Who or what was safer no because this man in his human weakness had been forced to humiliate himself? What truth had been enhanced by all this anguish?"

Miller himself was called to Washington and pressured to give HUAC more names, more people to ruin or to intimidate into confessions. He refused. His moral conviction made his meeting with Kazan all the more intense. The conversation of a man who bowed to the committee, and another who was determined to resist them was a drama as powerful as any either would place on the stage. It gave Miller the vision of what his play would be about: "the shifts of interests that turned loving husbands and wives into stony enemies, loving parents into indifferent supervisors or even exploiters of their children. As I already knew from my reading, that was the real story of ancient Salem Village, what they called the breaking of charity with one another."

Miller was again right. The break with charity is what drove the trials forward, as it did the HUAC hearings. It is what we must be on guard against today as we change laws to accommodate a state of war against terror. *The*

Crucible should be taught as fine writing, but also as an insight into how a witch-hunt works. When our comfort, safety, fear of being accused, and even justified anger at an enemy allows us to suppress doubt, and silence the voice of humanity that lets us identify with prisoners, suspects, and accused-evil-doers, then we are in real danger of doing evil ourselves. Miller's triumph was in creating a kind of psychological realism that did not depend at all on its historical setting. And that is how I think we should treat it today.

Miller has identified one more source for *The Crucible*, and that adds a final twist to this tangle of personal and national history, personal insight and literary accomplishment. At the Historical Society in Danvers he saw etchings of court scenes, perhaps from the trials. In the faces of the bearded judges recoiling from the agonized accusers he suddenly saw his own religious Jewish forebears. Salem was not just about America's Puritan, Protestant past; it was about "the moral intensity of the Jews and the clan's defensiveness against pollution from outside the ranks. I understood Salem in that flash, it was suddenly my own inheritance."

The Crucible is great because Miller penetrated the psychology of a political witch-hunt, and because it speaks about a moment in the life of a people aching to reach toward God and to protect themselves from evil. That, too, is in the headlines today. And a version of that same insight drew me to the Salem story. In the struggles of the Puritans to remain true to their faith in a time of increasing doubt, I saw my own grandfather, a leading Rabbi in Kiev, none of whose ten children were devout. This association made me sympathetic to the strains the Puritans experienced, while, for Miller, it explained their ferocious intensity.

If fiction can give us insights that transcend time—offering us a picture of the witch-hunt mentality that was true of the 1950s America in which it was written, the seventeenth-century Salem it describes, and is a caution to us in the twenty-first century—history can do something else. History sensitizes us to the subtle differences between time periods. The more we know about witchcraft beliefs in the seventeenth century the less they resemble the sexually driven fears and passions of *The Crucible*. On the other hand, though, as we study the objects and records left behind from the past, we make sense of them by examining our own ideas, memories, and images. We see ourselves through the past, and the past through ourselves. In the process both are modified. Being the product of the great struggle over modernization in Judaism made the struggles over modernization in the seventeenth century much more interesting to me, as it did for Miller.

History is a mirror, fiction a portrait. If Miller's painting has a few characters wrong, it still shows a great deal of truth, and his images are as resonant in the twenty-first century as they were fifty years ago. That is a great accomplishment, and should give classrooms much to talk about for generations to come.

Timeline of Milestones in Puritan History

Important Dates in Puritan History Before 1692

England
1535 King Henry VIII of England becomes head of the Church of
     England
1559 Book of Common Prayer adopted; Puritans find it too
     conservative
1590 Several Puritan leaders arrested

New World
1597 Protestant colony at mouth of St. Lawrence River fails

England
1603 James I becomes king, threatens Puritans

New World
1608 Scrooby congregation, future Pilgrims, leaves England
     for Amsterdam, Holland
1620 Mayflower Compact and Pilgrim settlement in Plymouth

England
1625 Charles I succeeds his father, James I

New World
1626 Roger Conant establishes English settlement at Salem

England
1628 William Laud, opponent of the Puritans, becomes bishop
     of London

New World

1629 Salem Covenant

1630 The "Great Migration" begins. In a decade, over 15,000
settlers, many of them Puritans, move to New England
from England

1636 Puritans fight against Pequots

England

1642 Civil War begins in England, King Charles I against
Parliament and Puritans

1646 Parliament defeats King Charles
Start of Quaker movement

1648 King escapes; war begins again

1649 King Charles executed

1653 Oliver Cromwell, a Puritan, becomes Lord Protector of the
Commonwealth England

New World

1656 Quakers arrive in Massachusetts, banished

1657 Massachusetts leaders adopt more lenient rules allowing
children of church members to become halfway members
even if they are not certain of being saved

1658 Death penalty instituted for Quakers

England

1658 Cromwell dies; struggle for succession

1660 Charles II crowned king; some Puritan leaders escape
to New England

New World

1661 Charles forbids execution of Quakers in Massachusetts

1675 Wampanoags under Metacom (King Philip) attack, start
of King Philip's War

1676–78 Metacom and allies defeated; heavy losses on both
sides In what is now Maine bloody clashes between
Wabanaki and New Englanders last until treaty of
April 1678

1684 Massachusetts Charter rescinded

England

1685 James II succeeds Charles II

New World

1686 Sir Edmund Andros named governor of New England

1688 Goodwin children afflicted

    War begins again in Maine area in which Wabanaki and
        French clash with New Englanders

England

1688 William of Orange invades and replaces James II

1689 William and Mary crowned

    Parliament passes act in favor of religious freedom

New World

1689 Colonists depose and imprison Andros

    Reverend Samuel Parris comes to Salem

1691 William Phips named governor of Massachusetts

Chronology of Events in the Salem Witch Crisis
1692

January	Elizabeth Parris, Abigail Williams, and Ann Putnam Jr. show strange behaviors
February	Mary Sibley organizes use of witch cake ritual; Tituba, Sarah Good, Sarah Osborne identified as witches
March 1	First examination; Tituba confesses
March 12	Martha Corey accused
March 19	Rebecca Nurse accused
March 21	Martha Corey examined
Late March	John and Elizabeth Proctor denounced
April 11	Deputy Governor Thomas Danforth leads examination of accusers
April 19	Abigail Hobbs, Bridget Bishop, Giles Corey, and Mary Warren examined
April 22– May 20	Fifteen suspected witches examined, including Mary Easty
	George Burroughs arrested in Maine; Margaret Jacobs confesses to being a witch
May 14	Increase Mather and William Phips, the new governor, arrive from England
May 18	Roger Toothaker arrested
May 27	Governor Phips creates the court of Oyer and Terminer to hear witchcraft cases

June 2	Bridget Bishop tried and convicted
June 10	Bishop hanged
June 15	Cotton Mather writes letter expressing ministers' concerns about use of invisible evidence
June 16	Roger Toothaker dies in prison
June 29–30	Rebecca Nurse, Susannah Martin, Sarah Wildes, Sarah Good, and Elizabeth How convicted
July 19	Nurse, Martin, Wildes, Good, and How hanged
Mid–July	Two accusers invited to Andover and new accusations begin; Minister Samuel Willard condemns the trials
August 2–6	George Jacobs, Martha Carrier, George Burroughs, John and Elizabeth Proctor, and John Willard convicted; Elizabeth is pregnant and her execution is delayed
August 19	George Jacobs, Carrier, Burroughs, John Proctor, and John Willard hanged
September 9	Martha Corey, Mary Easty, Alice Parker, Ann Pudeator, Dorcas Hoar, and Mary Bradbury convicted; Hoar confesses and is spared; Bradbury escapes
September 17	Margaret Scot, Wilmot Redd, Samuel Wardwell, Mary Parker, Abigail Faulkner, Rebecca Eames, Mary Lacy, and Abigail Hobbs convicted; Faulkner temporarily spared due to pregnancy; Eames, Lacy, and Hobbs executions delayed
September 19	Giles Corey pressed to death for refusing to make a plea
September 22	Martha Corey, Easty, Alice Parker, Pudeator, Scot, Redd, Wardwell, and Mary Parker are hanged
Early October	Increase Mather speaks against invisible evidence, convinces Phips to end the trials
Late October	Phips dissolves the court of Oyer and Terminer

1693

January–February	Trials begin again, but Phips does not allow the judges to hang even convicted witches
Spring–Summer	Phips requests pardons for even jailed and confessed witches; London agrees
August	Samuel Parris requests forgiveness for his mistakes

1696

Samuel Willard asks the colony to request God's forgiveness

1697

Samuel Sewall asks Minister Willard to read his confession in church

Joseph Green takes over church in Salem Village, heals community

Excommunication of Martha Corey rescinded

1699

War between Wabanaki and New Englanders ends

1706

Ann Putnam Jr. prepares confession for Green to read to congregation

Notes and Comments

The notes in the epilogue give readers a map to some of the trends in interpreting the trials. Here I present specific sources I have called on for facts, interpretations, quotations, and general background. While it has been useful to me to have to check and confirm that I have used each source correctly, and while I have provided accurate citations that readers can use, the notes are not primarily here as proof that I actually did research this book. Rather, they are meant to give readers a chance to move on from my work to other studies that have a great deal to offer. All of these are books written for adult readers, on the college or graduate school level. For that reason I indicate how accessible each one is for a younger reader. I urge readers to start with some of the more readable secondary books before tackling the primary sources, or to dip into the original documents to get a taste and flavor of the time and the people, but not to attempt to interpret them without first learning more about Puritan New England.

Note to the Reader

p. x The story of the lingering myths of Salem—how they took hold, were then debunked, and yet live on as undead, seemingly immortal wraiths—is itself a fascinating tale. Chadwick Hansen was a professor of English, and he took a fresh look at histories of the Salem trials in his *Witchcraft at Salem* (see especially the preface, pp. ix–xv). The book presents an easy overview of the views of previous historians. Though written for adults, Hansen's text is clear and straightforward. He exposed one set of myths and errors. While appreciating aspects of Hansen's scholarship, a second professor of English, Bernard Rosenthal, in *Salem Story* (hereafter *SS*), fundamentally disagrees with Hansen's basic conclusions (see p. 236 n. 29). Throughout the book, Rosenthal surveys the main views of Salem since 1969, as well as many fictional treatments, including those written for younger readers. Rosenthal's book has a slightly more scholarly tone in places than Hansen's, but his inclusion of TV accounts and books for young readers, his clear thinking, and his at times entertaining frustration with other scholars should appeal to motivated readers. Taken together, Hansen and Rosenthal map out how views of Salem have changed from the time of the trials to the present, though Mary Beth Norton's 2002 book, *In the Devil's Snare* (hereafter *DS*), suggests new directions for the future.

It is interesting that both *Witchcraft at Salem* and *Salem Story*— two of the books that have done the most to uncover errors in existing work—were by people who were not primarily students of colonial history. This is not to fault historians, but rather to suggest that in a case such as Salem, where there are limited sources and so much work has already been done, it sometimes takes an outsider with a fresh point of view to notice what others have missed. This should also be encouraging to young readers, for it means that if you spend the time to read the sources and the historical background, you, too, may have fresh insights to offer.

p. xi Exposing the mythologies around Tituba began with Hansen. Though he is best known for claiming there were real witches in Salem, he was also the first to show how Tituba had been transformed by later writers from an Indian slave into an African one and from being the first person accused to being the cause of the accusers' convulsions (see also his "The Metamorphosis of Tituba"). Rosenthal too summarizes the ways in which Tituba has been both mischaracterized and wrongly blamed (or credited) for bringing her native witchcraft to Salem in *SS,* pp. 10–14. I discuss the confusing beginning of the accusations in Salem in chapter II.

p. xi To get a good sense of what scholars now know about New England folk beliefs and magic, see Richard Godbeer's *The Devil's Dominion: Magic and Religion in Early New England* (hereafter

DD), pp. 7–23. Godbeer defines *magic* as a belief that humans can use occult means to influence the world, whereas *religion* involves a belief in a higher power to whose laws and rules humans must submit. In seventeenth-century New England, Godbeer thinks, these belief systems overlapped within individuals who were able to use magical practices in one moment and be sincerely devout in another. This is a study aimed at the college level, and younger readers may find it most useful by consulting the two indexes (one for names, the other for subjects) and by dipping in to learn more about a topic they have already begun to investigate in other, more easily accessible sources.

For one well-written study that shows this mixing of beliefs in both magic and religion in practice, see David D. Hall's *Worlds of Wonder, Days of Judgment* (hereafter *WW*), especially chapter 5, "The Mental World of Samuel Sewall," (pp. 213–238). Hall writes easily for a general adult audience, and the cited chapter in particular is so full of interesting details taken from Sewall's diary that it should appeal to many readers. Hall reads Sewall's diary as an anthropologist might if he were visiting and studying a very different culture. That approach in itself is fascinating.

p. xi The well-defined beliefs and practices of modern Wicca do not resemble the jumble of beliefs Godbeer and Hall describe. Still, Godbeer points out that the evidence we have of folk beliefs tends to come from court records and ministers' warnings, which is to say we learn about them when they are being condemned. Popular religion, folk magic, and the clashes and mixtures between these practices, as well as the fine words of highly trained ministers, are areas of study that continue to attract scholars.

p. xii This description of Salem is based on a personal visit on August 18, 2001. Rosenthal describes an earlier phase in which the city officially embraced a link to modern witchcraft, in *SS,* pp. 204–207.

On Spelling, Word Usage, and Dates in This Book

p. xv The current standard edition of the pretrial transcripts is Paul Boyer and Stephen Nissenbaum's edited *The Salem Witchcraft Papers* (hereafter *SWP*). There are three volumes in the edition, and when I cite them below, I indicate the volume number and the page number(s). The sample quotation in this section, selected almost at random, is from vol. 3, p. 788; you will find similar language, spelling, and punctuation on any page. You can also access *SWP* at http://etext.virginia.edu/salem/witchcraft. This Web site offers searchable texts of many primary sources related to the trials, and any student who wants to work from original materials will find it immensely valuable.

SWP is based on a compilation made in 1938, and scholars have since found errors in it, as well as a smattering of previously unknown documents. The biggest problem with it for anyone wanting to write a new view of the trials is that it is organized alphabetically by the name of the accused. The actual hearings, of course, took place over time and people with every name were shuffled together. While the editors list other relevant cases at the start of one person's testimony, the only real way to piece together all the testimonies that are linked to a case is to make your own chronology and skip back and forth in the transcripts. Like many other readers, I had to do just that, relying on sequences crafted by previous historians. But the problem is that until you have read all the testimonies, you cannot be sure what tiny nugget in one might be crucial for understanding another. Mary Beth Norton prepared a very extensive chronology and map of her own, and she says that helped a great deal in giving her new insights into the story (see her "Finding the Devil in the Details of the Salem Witchcraft Trials"). Bernard Rosenthal is now preparing a new edition of the transcripts; when it becomes available, it is sure to be a more reliable and useful resource than the original. And, to everyone's relief, it will be organized chronologically.

Introduction

p. 3 The subhead "The Queen of Hell" is from Cotton Mather's description of Martha Carrier; see Larry Gragg's *The Salem Witch Crisis* (hereafter *SWC*), p. 108. I find Gragg's book the best, most reliable overview of the story and recommend it for anyone wanting to get to know the whole episode in detail. Rosenthal discusses the source and implication of the label "queen of hell" in *SS,* p. 124.

p. 3 The court scene presented here follows directly from the transcript in Boyer and Nissenbaum, *SWP,* vol. 1, p. 185; I have added identifiers for the speakers. In the transcript the scribe erratically mixes past and present tense, dialogue and summary. I have very slightly paraphrased his past-tense summaries as part of the italicized passages and have recast them in the present tense.

The description of the accusers' bones as nearly coming apart can be found in *SWP,* vol. 1, p. 196. Goody Carrier's history of troubles is outlined in Gragg, *SWC,* p. 106.

p. 4 In *DS* Norton argues that the "black man" Susan claims to see was not primarily a reference to a diabolical person in black clothing, but rather to an evil, dark-skinned, Indian-like being (pp. 58–59, 343–44 n. 33). That was not my sense in reading the transcripts, but I have not studied this issue closely enough to be sure, and the argument is really part of Norton's larger, and surely accurate, sense of how the background of Indian wars influenced what people saw and said in Salem.

p. 8 For Sarah Carrier see Boyer and Nissenbaum, *SWP,* vol. 1, pp. 201–202.

p. 10 For the overwhelming tendency to accuse women as witches, see John Putnam Demos's *Entertaining Satan* (hereafter *ES*), p. 60. This is a scholarly book and is not directly about Salem at all. Still, Demos has thought deeply about witchcraft in seventeenth-century New England, and his insights are excellent preparation for anyone serious about studying Salem. In particular, he has done more to speculate on and attempt to define the psychology—the inner fears and stresses—reflected in witchcraft accusations than any other scholar of this period (see, the "Psychology" section, pp. 97–212). Some historians feel that there is not enough evidence to understand the unconscious mental conflicts of the time, but even if that is so, Demos's attempt is fascinating, and for the kind of reader who enjoys pondering the workings of the mind, it is worth reading as a kind of historical fiction.

The most extensive discussion of the striking gender imbalance in accusations of witchcraft is in Carol Karlsen's *The Devil in the Shape of a Woman,* pp. 46–76. Though her book is aimed at an academic audience, Karlsen writes well and has a clear and easy-to-follow point of view. She was the first to define a *witch* not as an unpopular, angry, or marginal woman, but rather as a woman whose inheritance of property disturbed men (see pp. 84–101). Karlsen's work is popular in colleges, and readers who are drawn to an analysis that uses the status of women as a key to understanding this particular time and place may well think she has gotten to the heart of the Salem outbreak. There have been challenges to Karlsen's conclusions, though, which she discusses with more vigor than grace in the afterword to the 1998 paperback edition of the book (see pp. 259–265).

p. 11 On witchcraft accusations of unpopular people, see *ES,* pp. 86–94, in which Demos creates a kind of "collective portrait" of a typical witch from the 114 cases he surveys, excluding those accused in Salem. (As we will see, though it started out as a typical outbreak, Salem departed from the patterns of other cases.)

For the theory that people accused those whom they had refused to help of being witches, see Keith Thomas, *Religion and the Decline of Magic,* p. 552. Thomas studied England, not New England; his lengthy book is aimed at the college level, and by now his key insights have been incorporated into (or dismissed by) more accessible and relevant studies of Salem. Nonetheless, the many cases he discusses are worth reading in their own right, and anyone who wants a broader background before reading about Salem would do well to use his extensive index and browse his pages.

On the association between witchery and outspokenness see Jane Kamensky, *Governing the Tongue,* pp. 151–53. This too is an academic study, but it is important as a leading example of the new generation of historians looking at Salem in ways that blend feminism, anthropology, and close attention to language.

p. 12 For the relevance of the Cinderella tale to witchcraft and to Salem in particular, see Paul Boyer and Stephen Nissenbaum, *Salem Possessed* (hereafter *SP*), p. 144. Readable, informative, and more broad-ranging than its title would suggest, this is an excellent short book that has become a standard title in any reading on Salem. It, too, has its detractors, who are more interested, for example, in the female accusers than in the males whose disputes, Boyer and Nissenbaum claim, were behind the trials. But it is a very good first step into more challenging books for a reader who wants to tackle college-level texts. I found the analogies to fairy tales simply brilliant.

pp. 12–13 For the Elizabeth Knapp story see Demos, *ES,* p. 103; for the idea that she might have been turning Willard, her protector, into a reverse image of the devil, see pp. 118–19.

p. 13 Phoebe's quotes are found in Boyer and Nissenbaum, *SWP,* vol. 1, pp. 191–92.

p. 14 For details on Benjamin Abbot see Boyer and Nissenbaum, *SWP,* vol. 1, p. 189.

pp. 17–18 On the kinds of evidence used in witchcraft cases, see Godbeer, *DD,* pp. 158–78, and Richard Weisman, *Witchcraft, Magic, and Religion in 17th-Century Massachusetts,* pp. 98–114. Weisman's study is written for scholars, but it is one of a cluster of books, with those of Godbeer, Demos, Boyer and Nissenbaum, Rosenthal, and Karlsen, that is part of any college reading list on Salem, as I'm sure Norton's *DS* will soon be as well. David Thomas Konig's *Law and Society in Puritan Massachusetts* is also part of this group of standard texts. Calling on close legal readings as well as anthropological insights, and based on the assumption that the law is used to control social conflict,

Konig's work is very useful for understanding the legal practices of the trials within the context of Massachusetts history.

Prologue

p. 23 A number of scholars have combed through the writings on witchcraft in seventeenth-century New England and have provided students and scholars with easy access to the original sources on episodes such as the Goodwin case. One such compilation, edited and with an introduction by David D. Hall, is *Witch-Hunting in Seventeenth-Century New England* (hereafter *WH*); for Cotton Mather on "bad language," see p. 268 of this volume. This is an excellent place to start research on attitudes and opinions expressed at the time and to see the Salem episode in the context of witchcraft cases throughout the century. A treasure trove for anyone seriously studying Salem is George Lincoln Burr's edited collection *Narratives of the Witchcraft Cases, 1648–1706* (hereafter *NWC*); for Mather on "heart of stone," see p. 100. Burr's collection contains contemporary writing by participants, defenders, and critics of the trials and provides a handy way to go beyond the snippets and quotations in books such as mine to get a real feel of the voices of the time. Be aware, though, that this is an anthology, and Burr sometimes includes only a part of a longer piece that you have to track down elsewhere. This collection is also available at http://etext.Virginia.edu/salem/witchcraft (the same site that hosts *SWP*).

p. 24 I am grateful to Professor Rosenthal for reminding me of the uncertainty over Glover's first name.

p. 24 For the sighting of the strange creature see Mather in Hall, *WH*, p. 271; for the children's relapse, see p. 270.

p. 25 For Nathaniel Hawthorne's description of this ritual at the meetinghouse, see his short story "Endicott and the Red Cross" in *Twice-Told Tales*, vol. 2, which is available at http://online-literature.com/hawthorne/133, or simply use a search engine and look for terms such as "Hawthorne," "Twice-Told," and "Red Cross" to find the story.

p. 26 On the Puritan family see Francis J. Bremer, *The Puritan Experiment;* pp. 113–15. This is a useful and informed survey book from the 1970s, brought up-to-date in a revised edition with ideas from more recent scholarship. While this history was once central to the U.S. history students learned from grade school on, much of it is now unfamiliar, especially the details of religious life, and Bremer offers a handy way to catch up on the basics.

pp. 27–28 On the Puritan imagery of pilgrimage see Charles E.

Hambrick-Stowe, *The Practice of Piety*, especially chapter 3, "Puritan as Pilgrim," (pp. 54–90). This is tough going for all young readers, except perhaps those who are studious and devout Protestants and are already familiar with the terms and concepts the author discusses. The ideas themselves, though, are fascinating. In *Holy War and the Promised Land* (New York: Clarion, 2004), the second book in the trilogy I began with *Sir Walter Ralegh and the Quest for El Dorado* (New York: Clarion, 2000), I discuss these themes in more detail.

p. 28 On this point about scalps see James Duncan Phillips, *Salem in the Eighteenth Century*, p. 58. This is historical writing of another era, and Phillips has little trouble defending the Puritans and generally painting the Indians as savage. Given that, and the fact that Phillips is vague about his own sources, I cannot be sure that the Puritans actually offered bounties for scalps. But since Phillips is, if anything, biased in favor of the Puritans, it seems likely.

p. 29 On the devil's promises see Hall, *WW*, p. 145.

p. 30 For Mather's comment on the scary French see Christine Leigh Heyrman, *Commerce and Culture* (hereafter *CC*), p. 106. This is a well-written and informative study that rewards the curious reader. Heyrman has traced the Quaker connection to the Salem outbreak and offers many other revealing details of colonial life. This study is rather more accessible and balanced than some of the other scholarship on this period.

p. 31 Details on the witch-protection tree are from Sidney Perley's *The History of Salem, Massachusetts*, p. 295, published in 1928. This multivolume work is history from another era, concerned with civic pride and carrying an assumption that the reader already knows and cares about the basic story. It is useful only either to get a taste of a very different style of writing and thinking or to cull for examples of local customs, such as this one.

p. 32 For Mather's often quoted line on "little sorceries," see his *Magnalia Christi Americana*, vol. 1, p. 205, easily available at www.graveworm.com/occult/texts/mathers.html, or by using a search engine to look for terms such as "Mather" and "little sorceries." For the longer quote see Weisman, *Witchcraft, Magic, and Religion in 17th-Century Massachusetts*, p. 60. For the rules of the scissors and sieve divination, see Thomas, *Religion and the Decline of Magic*, p. 213.

pp. 33–34 For Mather testing Glover and the discovery of the puppets, see Hall, *WH*, p. 270.

p. 35 On the "sad fits" of the children see Hall, *WH*, p. 273.

p. 36 For the quote on the "obnoxious woman" see Hall, *WH,* p. 273.

pp. 36–37 For flying and other torments see Hall, *WH,* pp. 274–75. For Mather on Martha and her struggles under his care, see Burr, *NWC,* p. 112.

pp. 37–38 For Goodwin's conclusion, as well as his specific comments about "bodies," "doctors," and "tricks," see Hall, *WH,* pp. 276–77, 279.

p. 39 For Mather's interest in using the Goodwin case as a warning against Quakers, see Heyrman, *CC,* p. 110.

p. 39 For Glover's "saints" see Hall, *WH,* p. 272; for the view on her Catholicism, see Karlsen, *Devil in the Shape of a Woman,* p. 34. Robert Calef, the great opponent of Mather and skeptic on the Salem trials, reports that Glover was known to be mentally unstable (see Burr, *NWC,* p. 124 n. 1). As to the Goodwin children in rebellion, see Hall, *WH,* p. 265.

Chapter I

p. 44 The first Salem Covenant is from Richard Gildrie, *Salem, Massachusetts, 1626–1683,* p. 170. This is an academic study that is most useful for those who have read Boyer and Nissenbaum's *SP* and want to know more about the tensions in Salem.

pp. 44–45 For Sewall see Hall, *WW,* p. 227; for the woman from Wenham, see *WW,* p. 123; and for Anne Fitch, see *WW,* p. 136.

p. 45 For a wonderful, accessible book on this "visible saint" aspect of Puritanism, see Edmund Morgan's *Visible Saints.* Morgan writes for college-level readers, but any motivated high school student will find his study a useful resource.

p. 46 On the Puritan "relation" and how it worked in a congregation, see Bremer, *The Puritan Experiment,* p. 110.

p. 46 For this quote encapsulating the Puritan mission, see Hall, *WW,* p. 150.

pp. 46–47 The history of the Putnams, including their holdings, is from Boyer and Nissenbaum, *SP,* pp. 111, 123, 125–26, 136.

pp. 47–48 For the history of the Porters see Boyer and Nissenbaum, *SP,* pp. 117–18.

pp. 48–49 On the economic shift in Salem in general, and on the merchant class as a distinct group, see Gildrie, *Salem, Massachusetts, 1626–1683*, pp. 122, 172. The hostility that communities bound together in faith may feel toward the individualism and lack of boundaries of the outside world continues to this day. Some experts on tensions between Western countries and Islamic fundamentalists see this as a crucial issue dividing the two societies.

pp. 49–50 For the two warring families' characteristics see Boyer and Nissenbaum, *SP*, p. 115.

pp. 50–51 On this history of the Putnams—the different generations, the marriages, Thomas Sr.'s second family, and his contested will—as well as on the likeness of the drama to fairy tales, see Boyer and Nissenbaum, *SP*, pp. 135–38, 143.

pp. 52–53 On the story of Salem Village's background—particularly its fight to have its own church and minister outlined here—several sources are available, among them Charles W. Upham's two-volume work, *Salem Witchcraft* (hereafter *SW*), which was first published in 1867 and which was often used by historians of an earlier era. Upham provides no notes or references, but he began writing about the trials in the 1830s, lived in Salem amid the descendants of the accused and accusers, and is our only source for the kind of oral history, gossip, and physical detail that remains in the memory of a town long after an event. When it is possible to compare his text to other sources, he is sometimes accurate and sometimes not.

A completely different kind of book about the same subject matter is Bryan F. Le Beau's *The Story of the Salem Witch Trials* (hereafter *SWT*). This is a survey of the trials as well as historical scholarship on them, written for college courses. It is a concise and relatively thorough book that is useful as a kind of baseline summary of what happened in 1692 and what people think about it now. Unfortunately, though, the author sometimes cites rather questionable secondary books, such as Marion Starkey's *The Devil in Massachusetts*, instead of the original source he presumably used, and there are also small errors in other citations that make it difficult to follow the trail of his research. I recommend using *SWT* to get basic information but double-checking details against works by other historians.

For Le Beau's version of James Bayley's story see *SWT*, pp. 53–54. Upham recounts the story of the death of Bayley's wife in *SW*, p. 237. For details on Samuel Parris, see Boyer and Nissenbaum, *SP*, pp. 152–67, especially pp. 162–63; and for a wonderful, careful reading of Parris's sermons, see pp. 168–71 of *SP*.

Chapter II

pp. 58–60 For John Hale's essay see Burr, *NWC*, p. 425. For his quote on the egg white see Hansen, *Witchcraft at Salem*, p. 30, for although Hale's report is reprinted in *NWC*, this section is omitted. To see the original, go to http://etext.virginia.edu/salem/witchcraft. There, if you search for Hale's "Modest Inquiry on the Nature of Witchcraft," you will find a facsimile of the essay, with the quotation on pp. 132–33.

p. 59 For information on Betty see Larry Gragg, *A Quest for Security*, p. 117. This is a useful scholarly book for those who want to understand more about the minister who was at the center of the outbreak. As for Abigail, for a completely speculative description of her fate based on Hale's clue, see Frances Hill, *A Delusion of Satan*, p. 215. Though vividly written, I found this book unreliable and simplistic in its understanding of the Puritans. Norton speculates that Hale may have been referring to Susannah Sheldon, not Abigail Williams, because Sheldon died early and unmarried, five years after the trials (see *DS,* p. 311).

p. 60 For Cole, see Boyer and Nissenbaum, *SWP,* vol. 1, p. 228.

pp. 60–61 For Hale's description of the afflicted girls see Burr, *NWC,* p. 413; for Calef's see *NWC,* p. 342. This is one of the joys of using Burr's collection: You can leap back and forth from one account to another, almost hearing the different speakers making their cases to you, interpreting the same moment in very different ways.

p. 63 For Ann Putnam Sr. see Upham, *SW,* vol. 1, pp. 69–70, 237. Upham's portrait of her was based on local traditions, which may well have been true, but at this date they are also impossible to confirm. Spiritualism was both popular and controversial in Upham's day, and he might have been reading a current preoccupation back into the historical record.

pp. 65–67 Elaine G. Breslaw has made the most extensive effort to date to determine who Tituba may have been, as well as to set the fragmentary details we know about her in a broader context of studies of Puritans, slavery, and Caribbean Indians at the time; see her *Tituba, Reluctant Witch of Salem.* This is academic research, but it is full of anthropological details that a young reader interested in the subject is sure to find fascinating. The most exciting discovery consists of two versions of lists of slaves on a Barbados plantation in 1676. Both include a young person named Tattuba, and one also includes a boy named John (see photos on pp. 64 and 65). This could be a record of Tituba and John Indian before Parris purchased them. For a shorter version of Breslaw's views, in a useful anthology of primary sources and subsequent interpretations, see her "Tituba's Confession," pp. 444–53. Breslaw's work is most useful as a portrait of what we know about beliefs and practices in Tituba's age. We just do not have enough evidence to link that general knowledge to the actual person.

p. 67 For the history of the Tituba myth see Rosenthal, *SS,* pp. 10–14.

p. 67 For two versions of the rye cake test see Hale (p. 413) and Calef (p. 342), both in Burr, *NWC*. In a note on p. 342 Burr also cites Parris's account of the rye cake test in his own church record. Rosenthal weighs out the different stories, including a more thorough reading of Parris's record, and emphasizes Mary Sibley's role in *SS*, pp. 26–27; I am grateful to him for reminding me that, while it is tempting to say the test led to the girls' naming Tituba, the actual record does not make that direct link.

p. 68 For Hale on Tituba's English mistress being a witch, see Burr, *NWC*, p. 414.

p. 68 For Breslaw's research and speculations on the type of Indian Tituba may have been, see *Tituba, Reluctant Witch of Salem*, pp. 9–14.

pp. 69–70 For the rumor about the French Catholics inciting the Indians, see Phillips, *Salem in the Eighteenth Century*, p. 47. Godbeer in *DD* (p. 200) stresses the colonists' fears of Indians. The quote about the "tawny man" is from Boyer and Nissenbaum, *SWP*, vol. 3, p. 768. And for Mather's quotes on the Indians, see Godbeer, *DD*, pp. 192–93.

p. 70 In *DS* Norton explores the effect of the Indian wars on a number of the girls and women who were among the most active accusers in the Salem trials (see appendix II, pp. 319–20, for a list of those linked to the Indian wars).

pp. 71–72 For Parris blaming Sibley, see Gragg, *SWC*, p. 69. For the story of Parris beating Tituba, see Calef in Burr, *NWC*, p. 343. In *Tituba, Reluctant Witch of Salem* Breslaw inexplicably assumes Parris beat Tituba to force her to confess to having conducted the test rather than confess to being a witch (p. 109), which does not fit Calef's account at all. Covering the same events in "Tituba's Confession" (p. 449), however, she gets it right. Breslaw is good at analyzing who had what at stake in Calef's story about Parris beating Tituba (see *Tituba, Reluctant Witch of Salem*, p. 223 n. 5).

p. 72 For Parris's warning on using the devil's tools against him, see Gragg, *SWC*, p. 69.

p. 73 Godbeer notes that people in the Salem area in this period were particularly ready to blame others rather than investigate their own errors in *DD*, p. 203.

Chapter III

pp. 77–78 Characterizations of Good and Osborne are from Gragg, *A Quest for Security*, pp. 113–14. Calef describes Good as "distracted" or melancholy in Burr, *NWC,* p. 343; and Rosenthal discusses Good's age in *SS,* pp. 87–88.

p. 78 For the judges see Gragg, *SWC,* p. 48.

p. 79 For moving the hearing to the meetinghouse and setting the scene, see Upham, *SW,* vol. 2, p. 12. This is the kind of wonderful detail Upham supplies, but for which he is the sole authority. Further details on the hearing in this section are also from Upham, *SW,* vol. 2, p. 35; it is impossible to know if his account is accurate, but what he says does not conflict with the recorded testimony. For the actual dialogue see Boyer and Nissenbaum, *SWP,* vol. 2, p. 358.

p. 81 For Osborne on the Indian image see Boyer and Nissenbaum, *SWP,* vol. 2, p. 611.

p. 81 For Tituba on Betty see Boyer and Nissenbaum, *SWP,* vol. 3, p. 753.

pp. 82–87 For Tituba's first responses see Boyer and Nissenbaum, *SWP,* vol. 3, p. 747; for Breslaw's analysis of Tituba's confession in the context of wider cultural studies, see *Tituba, Reluctant Witch of Salem,* pp.117–22. On the girls' pains ending upon the start of Tituba's confession, see *SWP,* vol. 3 p. 757. For Tituba's description of the devil's enticements, see *SWP,* vol. 3, p. 748.

pp. 83–84 For details on Tituba's dream—including her claim of flight, her travel to Boston, and the clothing she described—see Boyer and Nissenbaum, *SWP,* vol. 3, pp.749, 750, 753, 755. On the possible Indian origin for Tituba's belief in dream flight, see Breslaw, *Tituba, Reluctant Witch of Salem,* p. 127. Even today there is a degree of ambiguity in evaluating dream evidence. For example, when the "Dreamtime" of Australian Aborigines is discussed, we say it is real to them. If we grant that to them, there is no reason to be less accepting of the Puritans.

pp. 85–86 For Osborne's two creatures and Tituba's claim to have seen one of them the previous night, see Boyer and Nissenbaum, *SWP,* vol. 3, pp. 749, 752. For the *kenaima* theory see Breslaw, *Tituba, Reluctant Witch of Salem,* p. 128. For the devil's book, see *SWP,* vol. 3, p. 754.

pp. 86–87 For Tituba's claim of nine witches and their location, see Boyer and Nissenbaum, *SWP,* vol. 3, pp. 754–55.

p. 87 In contrast to my account in this chapter, Norton argues that the turning point of the trials was not Tituba's confession, but rather Abigail Hobbs's confession and Ann Putnam Jr.'s vision of the evil minister George Burroughs. She believes these events, which linked Salem to the attacks in Maine, led to the rapid increase in the number and scope of the accusations (see *DS,* p. 120).

Chapter IV

p. 91 For Ann's record in the trials see Rosenthal, *SS*, p. 41. On a recent internet search I saw an article that listed her as involved in eighteen of twenty-one deaths, but it did not give any particulars for the additional case (beyond the nineteen hangings and Giles Corey's death by torture), which is apparently a newly discovered account. Rosenthal's forthcoming edition of the trials is sure to include the most recent data on the number of trials, convictions, and deaths.

Throughout *DS* Norton argues that the most important accuser in the Salem witch trials was Mercy Lewis, not Ann Putnam Jr. Lewis lived in the Putnams' home, had direct links to the Maine disasters, and could have fed or influenced the Putnams (see especially pp. 134 and 137). I think, though, that Norton has done a better job of establishing Lewis's importance and motivations than of making sense of Ann Putnam Jr. This is the kind of historical quandary scholars will be debating for years to come, and any readers who want to be able to participate in that discussion should read Norton's book.

p. 92 For Ann's story about Dorothy Good's ghost see Boyer and Nissenbaum, *SWP,* vol. 1, p. 246, and vol. 2, p. 353; the word *throat* is my extrapolation from "almost choke" in the transcripts. For the Proctor story see *SWP,* vol. 2, p. 668.

Hansen argues that the accusers were in a state of true psychological torment, which fits the medical diagnosis of "hysteria." He finds a strong similarity between exactly the kind of symptoms Ann reported, such as choking and hallucinating, and case studies by famous analysts such as Sigmund Freud (see *Witchcraft at Salem,* p. 1). For Rosenthal's summary of the various schools of thought about what may have been afflicting the accusers, including the hysteria theory, see *SS,* pp. 32–36.

p. 94 For the story of the two men on the dark night, see Boyer and Nissenbaum, *SWP,* vol. 3, p. 371.

p. 95 For discussions of beliefs of thunder as a divine voice and as a natural event, see Hall, *WW,* pp. 76, 77, 78, 79, 106.

p. 96 For the theory that the Putnams were aiming at Mary Veren Putnam without entirely knowing it, see Boyer and Nissenbaum, *SP,* pp. 146–47.

p. 96 For Ann's accusation of Martha Corey see Boyer and Nissenbaum, *SWP,* vol. 1, p. 260.

p. 97 For Martha's test see Boyer and Nissenbaum, *SWP,* vol. 1, p. 261.

p. 98 On Mercy Lewis see Boyer and Nissenbaum, *SWP,* vol. 1, pp. 264–65.

p. 99 On Abigail Williams see Gragg, *SWC*, p. 57. Lawson's account of Abigail's possession and behavior appears in Burr, *NWC*, pp. 153–54.

p. 100 Godbeer discusses appreciatively but skeptically two different interpretations of afflicted young women as "acting out" (see *DD*, p. 111 n. 115 and p. 117 n. 139). As cited earlier in a note on p. 10, Demos, in *ES*, has made the most thorough effort to date to discern the inner conflicts of people in witchcraft cases based on their symptoms, as recorded in court records.

p. 100 For Lawson's account of his interrupted sermon, see Burr, *NWC*, p. 154.

Chapter V

pp. 105–106 For Hathorne's questioning of Martha see Boyer and Nissenbaum, *SWP*, vol. 1, p. 248; his quote about "terror to evil-doers" is on p. 251. Norton points out that judges at this time presumed the accused were guilty, and thus the Salem judges were not behaving in an unusual fashion (see *DS*, pp. 27–42). This does not contradict the prior record in which most people accused of witchcraft went free because judges alone did not render verdicts—juries did.

pp. 106–107 For Martha's claim of innocence and the crowd's reaction, see both Boyer and Nissenbaum, *SWP*, vol. 1, p. 248, and Lawson's rendition in Burr, *NWC*, p. 155. For her beginning to crack, see *SWP*, vol. 1, p. 250. For signs of "distraction" and all being against Martha, see *SWP*, vol. 1, p. 251.

p. 109 For Norton's speculation that the testimony of the young accusers was also echoed by written descriptions of their afflictions taken down by men but since lost, see *DS*, p. 72.

pp. 109–111 For the accusers calling out questions to Martha and the story about the pin, see Lawson's comments in Burr, *NWC*, p. 156, which are echoed by Calef in the same volume, on p. 344. For Ann Putnam's claims of Elizabeth How's use of a pin, see Rosenthal, *SS*, p. 36; Lawson's story about pins and bindings appears in Upham, *SW*, vol. 2, appendix, p. 530. For the story about Sheldon being tied up, see Boyer and Nissenbaum, *SWP*, vol. 2, pp. 370–71.

pp. 111–112 For the issue raised by the bites and pins see Rosenthal, *SS*, p. 36. For an instance of bite marks confirmed by the court, see Cotton Mather's *The Wonders of the Invisible World*, in Burr, *NWC*, pp. 216–17. For Calef's story about the knife see *NWC*, pp. 357–58.

pp. 112–113 For brooms and poles left in trees see Boyer and Nissenbaum, *SWP,* vol. 2, p. 371.

p. 113 The famous reference to "sport" is in Boyer and Nissenbaum, *SWP,* vol. 2, p. 665. It is not clear in what context or at what time the girl said this. In the transcript the unnamed girl says "she," not "I," but she is speaking about herself.

p. 114 The quote that comprises the subhead on this page is from Boyer and Nissenbaum, *SWP,* vol. 2, p. 585.

pp. 114–115 For general background information on the case of Rebecca Nurse, see Boyer and Nissenbaum, *SP,* p. 149; the conflict over the pigs is in Rosenthal, *SS,* p. 92. For the words of her supporters see Boyer and Nissenbaum, *SWP,* vol. 2, p. 594; but because this account of Rebecca's response to the accusations was from people who believed in her and were advocating for her, it may be doubted.

p. 116 Lawson's observation of Ann Sr. can be found in Burr, *NWC,* p. 157. The interpretation of Ann's struggle with the specter of Rebecca comes from Boyer and Nissenbaum, *SP,* pp. 148–49. Rosenthal, in an undated personal communication, strongly objects that Boyer and Nissenbaum's effort to glean Ann Putnam's subconscious intentions from her spoken words relies on a saintly image of Rebecca that was a nineteenth-century creation and employs a method of psychoanalysis that is simply inappropriate for seventeenth-century sources. I respect his caution but find their interpretation at least compelling as a speculation and possibly true.

pp. 116–117 The opening of the hearing is documented in Boyer and Nissenbaum, *SWP,* vol. 2, pp. 584–85.

pp. 117–118 For Ann Sr.'s claim of being attacked by "beasts," see Boyer and Nissenbaum, *SWP,* vol. 2, p. 605. Lawson's description of the scene from outside the courtroom is in Burr, *NWC,* p. 159; Lawson is explicit that this was a secondhand account, so the details may not be precise, but the overall effect he describes matches what is captured in the testimony.

pp. 118–119 For the dramatic exchanges between Hathorne and Nurse, see Boyer and Nissenbaum, *SWP,* vol. 2, pp. 586–87.

p. 119 For Nurse bringing up the devil using her likeness, see Boyer and Nissenbaum, *SWP,* vol. 2, p. 587.

p. 120 On Lawson and his sermon see Boyer and Nissenbaum, *SWP,* vol. 1, p. 164, and Gragg, *SWC,* p. 67.

pp. 120–121 On Parris's sermon see Gragg, *A Quest for Security,* pp. 123–24; his remark on covetousness is on p. 124.

p. 122 Lawson gives the version of Cloyce's departure that favors anger or guilt having caused the door to slam; ever the skeptic, Calef credits the wind (see Burr, *NWC,* pp. 161 and 346, respectively). This is another example of how useful Burr's collection is.

Chapter VI

p. 125 Samuel Sewall's quote that is used as the first subhead in this chapter is noted in many sources, including Gragg, *SWC,* p. 82.

p. 126 For the petition in support of Rebecca Nurse, see Boyer and Nissenbaum, *SWP,* vol. 2, pp. 592–93; we are not sure when this petition was submitted, though internal evidence suggests it was later in the summer, after she had been convicted. Doubts about Elizabeth Proctor's being accused are discussed in Gragg, *SWC,* p. 77.

p. 127 For Cloyce's response to John Indian and the overall courtroom scene here, see Boyer and Nissenbaum, *SWP,* vol. 2, p. 659.

p. 127 Lewis's testimony is in Gragg, *SWC,* p. 70.

pp. 128–29 For Danforth's challenges to both accused and accusers, see Boyer and Nissenbaum, *SWP,* vol. 2, pp. 659–60.

p. 129 For the spirits of the accused inhabiting the courtroom and the accusations against the Proctors, see Boyer and Nissenbaum, *SWP,* vol. 2, pp. 660–61.

pp. 130–31 Background on Phips and his comments on the colony upon his arrival there can be found in Burr, *NWC,* pp. 196, 199, and in Gragg, *SWC,* p. 86. An older view of Phips had it that he was preoccupied with military matters and was hardly involved with the witchcraft cases after he set up the court, which was the picture of him I initially painted. Rosenthal cautioned me that this was a myth crafted by Phips after the fact to protect himself, but it was only when I saw this interpretation restated in Norton's *DS* (pp. 237–38) that I corrected my text. I am grateful to both Rosenthal and Norton for saving me from perpetuating a mistaken view of Phips.

pp. 131–32 On Saltonstall see Gragg, *SWC,* p. 87; on his speedy resignation, see Rosenthal, *SS,* p. 233 n. 8. On Clinton see Boyer and Nissenbaum, *SWP,* vol. 1, p. 217.

pp. 132–33 For the argument that there was a skeptical mind-set at the time, see Rosenthal, *SS,* pp. 183–86. Questions about the physics of an accused witch's supposed ability to knock down her accusers by glancing at them were raised in a letter written by Thomas Brattle during the trials and later made public; it can be found in Burr, *NWC,* p. 171.

pp. 134–35 For Bridget Bishop see Boyer and Nissenbaum, *SWP,* vol. 1, p. 86.

p. 134 Rosenthal's *SS* gives various possible interpretations of the puppet story on p. 76.

p. 135 Calef tells the story of John's bite in Burr, *NWC,* p. 348.

pp. 135–36 The excerpts from Mather's report about the Bishop case are in Burr, *NWC,* pp. 223, 229.

p. 136 Brattle describes the charge to the jury in Burr, *NWC,* pp. 187–88.

p. 137 For "The Return of Several Ministers" see Gragg, *SWC,* pp. 101–102; the final paragraph wherein the ministers ultimately leave the matter to the judges is on p. 103.

pp. 138–39 The last paragraph of this chapter is the second occasion on which my original text followed an older, now clearly inaccurate interpretation, and the comments of Rosenthal and the example of Mary Beth Norton's *DS* caused me to revise my views. The older view held that the accusers began to "overreach" and make wild accusations, which brought them into conflict with powerful leaders who eventually ended the trials. One of Norton's breakthroughs has been to show that the accusations of figures such as John Alden and George Burroughs were directly linked to the Maine wars and made perfect sense in light of the influence of those attacks on the trials.

Chapter VII

pp. 143–44 For Ann's vision, including the ghosts of Burroughs's murdered wives, see Boyer and Nissenbaum, *SWP,* vol. 1, pp. 164, 166. For the dates of Burroughs's arrest and his arrival back in Salem, see *SWP,* vol. 1, p. 152.

p. 145 For belief in the idea that "murder will out," see Hall, *WW,* p. 176.

pp. 145–46 For details on the new arrests see Gragg, *SWC,* pp. 112–13. For Daniel Andrew in particular, who was never brought to trial, see Weisman, *Witchcraft, Magic, and Religion in 17th-Century Massachusetts,* appendix C, p. 109. I am grateful to Mary Beth Norton for correcting my account of these arrests. In describing some of the details, I have borrowed the wording in her note to me.

p. 146 Norton's more recent interpretation on the arrests of wealthy people is in *DS,* pp. 156–57.

p. 147 For the quote on "tingling" see Boyer and Nissenbaum, *SWP,* vol. 1, p. 165.

pp. 147–48 For Burroughs's physical appearance, his presumed strength, and his role as Mercy Lewis's tempter, see Boyer and Nissenbaum, *SWP,* vol. 1, pp. 167, 168-69, 170, 171.

p. 148 For Hobbs's testimony see Boyer and Nissenbaum, *SWP,* vol. 1, p. 173.

p. 148 On Burroughs's not baptizing all but one of his children, see Boyer and Nissenbaum, *SWP,* vol. 1, p. 153.

pp. 148–49 Cotton Mather's account of Burroughs's hearing— including the passages about Burroughs being a "conjurer," about promises he made, and about both the noise and the accusers' inability to speak in the courtroom—is in Burr, *NWC,* pp. 216, 217, 219; Mather quotes Burroughs citing the English book on p. 222.

p. 150 For the story about Margaret Jacobs visiting Burroughs, see Calef in Burr, *NWC,* p. 364, and Boyer and Nissenbaum, *SWP,* vol. 2, pp. 490–91.

pp. 150–51 Sources on Burroughs's execution are numerous: for Mather's account of Burroughs's death see Burr, *NWC,* p. 222; for opposing views on Burroughs see Calef in *NWC,* pp. 360–61; Brattle's comments are in *NWC,* p. 177; and Sewall's diary entry is found in Rosenthal, *SS,* p. 145. The idea of "two men in black" on Gallows Hill is from Calef in *NWC,* p. 177; Rosenthal cites two scholars who doubt Calef in *SS,* p. 249 n. 47.

pp. 152–53 The issue of Burroughs's possible abuse is summarized with quotations in Gragg, *SWC,* pp. 114–15.

Rosenthal speculates, while realizing there is only very frail evidence, that Ann Putnam Sr. might have beaten and murdered her child and that Ann transposed that into a vision of an accused witch whipping her to death (see *SS,* p. 40). For speculations on child abuse, or false accusations of child abuse, being an important clue in the Salem story, see Peter Charles Hoffer, *The Salem Witchcraft Trials*, pp. 49–50 and 79–80.

p. 153 Norton describes the 1676 attack that devastated Mercy Lewis's family in *DS,* pp. 48–50; Lewis's and Hobbs's Maine connections with Burroughs are discussed more generally on pp. 128–131.

Chapter VIII

pp. 155, 157 The title of this chapter and the title of the first subhead are from Margaret Jacobs in Boyer and Nissenbaum, *SWP,* vol. 2, p. 491.

pp. 157–58 On Abigail Hobbs see Boyer and Nissenbaum, *SWP,* vol. 2, p. 409.

p. 158 On Mary Warren see Rosenthal, *SS,* pp. 47–48.

p. 159 Norton offers her speculative identification of the two unnamed accusers who went to Andover in *DS,* p. 233.

pp. 159–60 For Sarah Churchill's story see Boyer and Nissenbaum, *SWP*, vol. 1, p. 211. Sarah Ingersoll's account of Churchill's confession is in the same volume, on pp. 211–12.

pp. 161–62 For Margaret Jacobs's recantation see Boyer and Nissenbaum, *SWP*, vol. 2, p. 491; her quote about seeing "nothing but death," is on pp. 491–92.

p. 162 A modern-day example of a person whose belief in speaking the truth has had important consequences is Vaclav Havel, former president of the Czech Republic. It may sound odd, or overstated, to compare the confessions of seventeenth-century admitted liars to people who have changed the fate of nations in our own time, but Havel's basic idea of "living in truth" animated his resistance to the Communist state, sustained him during his many imprisonments, and has a great deal in common with the realization Jacobs and Churchill came to that they simply could not bear lying. See Havel's *The Power of the Powerless* (New York: M. E. Sharpe, 1990).

p. 165 On Rebecca Nurse's jury reversing itself, see Calef in Burr, *NWC*, p. 358.

p. 165 The quote that forms this chapter subhead is from John Proctor's plea, discussed on the following pages, in Boyer and Nissenbaum, *SWP*, vol. 2, p. 689.

p. 166 For Proctor's plea see Boyer and Nissenbaum, *SWP*, vol. 2, pp. 689–90.

p. 167 The new theory that the judges felt vulnerable to criticism for the Indian attacks and thus more receptive to witchcraft accusations can be found in Norton, *DS*, p. 299. For the possibility that the judges were following English precedent in accepting torture, see Konig, *Law and Society in Puritan Massachusetts*, p. 172.

p. 169 The case against George Corwin is outlined in Rosenthal, *SS*, pp. 196–201, but Gragg is unconvinced that Corwin was actually profiting from the cases (compare with *SWC*, p. 103, and *SS*, p. 199). The Corwin/Jacobs family story is in *SWC*, p. 129.

pp. 170–71 Thomas Brattle's observations are in Burr, *NWC*, pp. 177–78. The information on the cases against Samuel Willard and John Hale's wife being summarily dismissed is from Rosenthal, *SS*, p. 178.

Chapter IX

p. 173 The title of this chapter is a quote from Mary Easty's final petition letter to the court, in Boyer and Nissenbaum, *SWP*, vol. 1, p. 304.

pp. 175–76 This exchange between Easty and the judge is in Boyer and Nissenbaum, *SWP,* vol. 1, p. 289.

pp. 176–77 The story of Easty's release and Mercy Lewis's fit is from Boyer and Nissenbaum, *SWP,* vol. 1, p. 301; for the accusers backing off, see p. 304. Rosenthal outlines the chronology of Mary's hearings in *SS,* p. 176.

p. 177 For Easty and Cloyce's joint petition to the judges, see Boyer and Nissenbaum, *SWP,* vol. 1, pp. 302–303.

pp. 179–80 For Easty's famous final letter see Boyer and Nissenbaum, *SWP,* vol. 1, pp. 304–305.

p. 181 The quote that comprises the subhead on this page is from Eunice Fry in Gragg, *SWC,* p. 164.

p. 181 Increase Mather's quotations are from Gragg, *SWC,* pp. 173–75.

pp. 182–83 Brattle's letter appears in Burr, *NWC,* p. 184.

pp. 182–83 Phips's letters to London are reproduced in Burr, *NWC,* pp. 196–97. Norton proves that Phips was aware of and involved in the trials in *DS,* p. 237; Rosenthal stressed this same point to me in a personal communication.

p. 183 Easty's "alteration" quote from her final petition, discussed earlier, is in Boyer and Nissenbaum, *SWP,* vol. 1, p. 304. As stated in the first note to this subsection, Eunice Fry was the woman who openly admitted that her confession "was all false." Phips's quotations are from his aforementioned letters to London, in Burr, *NWC,* p. 201.

p. 184 The last phase of the trials is described by Gragg in *SWC,* pp. 181–83.

p. 184 The subtitle's quote here is from Parris in Gragg, *SWC,* p. 184.

p. 185 For Parris's August 1693 sermon see Boyer and Nissenbaum, *SP,* pp. 176–77.

pp. 185–86 For Parris's 1694 confession see Gragg, *SWC,* pp. 184–85.

p. 186 For Sewall's statement on God's anger see Calef's proclamation in Burr, *NWC,* pp. 385–86.

p. 186 For Cotton Mather's diary entry see Rosenthal, *SS,* p. 202.

pp. 186–87 For Sewall's statement read in church see Gragg, *SWC,* p. 186.

p. 187 For the jury members' apology, see Calef in Burr, *NWC,* p. 387.

Chapter X

p. 189 The chapter title is from a quote by Ann Putnam Jr. in Upham, *SW,* vol 2, p. 110.

p. 191 Green's conciliatory skills are discussed by Upham in *SW,* vol. 2, pp. 506–508, and by Boyer and Nissenbaum in *SP,* pp. 218–19.

p. 192 Upham was unable to finally determine how many children Ann Jr. was responsible for upon her parents' death. On her age and her failing health see *SW,* vol. 2, p. 509; he says her health "began to decline and she was long an invalid," but it is not clear what that implies—chronic illness or some specific form of incapacity.

pp. 192–93 For Ann's confessional statement see Gragg, *SWC,* p. 187.

pp. 194–95 Thomas Putnam's odd-sounding letter is in Boyer and Nissenbaum, *SWP,* vol. 1, pp. 165, 166. See note above corresponding to p. 106 for Hathorne's use of the same phrase "terror to evil-doers."

p. 197 Norton outlines Lewis's later life in *DS,* on p. 310.

pp. 199–200 I discuss both the rebellious side of the 1960s and the recent continuities noted with the '50s in my *Art Attack: A Short Cultural History of the Avant-Garde* (New York: Clarion, 1998), pp. 123–33.

p. 202 For Putnam's "wheel" phrase, see Boyer and Nissenbaum, *SWP,* vol. 1, p. 165.

Appendix

p. 225 Miller's quote is from his autobiography, *Timebends,* p. 331.

p. 226 Miller, *Timebends,* p. 334.

p. 226 Miller, *Timebends,* p. 335.

p. 227 Miller, *Timebends,* p. 338.

Timeline

Puritan history follows a more extensive chronology in Bremer's, *The Puritan Experiment.* The timeline of Salem events is based on a similar and more complete version in Hoffer's *The Salem Witchcraft Trials.* In a few details Hoffer's chronology does not match that of Rosenthal in *SS;* in those cases, I have followed Rosenthal. I also consulted Marilynne K. Roach's *The Salem Witch Trials* for the chronology of events. Dates for the Indian clashes in Maine are from Norton's *DS,* but even many of the dates in that drama are subject to debate, so it is always worthwhile to check multiple sources against one another.

Bibliography

Boyer, Paul, and Stephen Nissenbaum. *Salem Possessed: The Social Origins of Witchcraft* (Cambridge, MA: Harvard University Press, 1974); abbreviated in the "Notes" as *SP*.

——, eds. *The Salem Witchcraft Papers.* 3 vols. (New York: Da Capo Press, 1977); abbreviated in the "Notes" as *SWP*.

Bremer, Francis J. *The Puritan Experiment: New England Society from Bradford to Edwards* (New York: St. Martin's Press, 1976; rev. ed., Hanover, NH: University Press of New England, 1995) (page citations are to the 1995 edition).

Breslaw, Elaine G. *Tituba, Reluctant Witch of Salem: Devilish Indians and Puritan Fantasies* (New York: New York University Press, 1996).

——. "Tituba's Confession: The Multicultural Dimensions of the 1692 Salem Witch-Hunt." In Elaine Breslaw, ed., *Witches of the Atlantic World: A Historical Reader and Primary Sourcebook* (New York: New York University Press, 2000).

Burr, George Lincoln, ed. *Narratives of the Witchcraft Cases, 1648–1706* (New York: Charles Scribner's Sons, 1914; reprint, New York: Barnes and Noble, 1968) (page citations are to the 1968 edition); abbreviated in the "Notes" as *NWC*.

Carlson, Laurie Winn. *A Fever in Salem: A New Interpretation of the New England Witch Trials* (Chicago: Ivan R. Dee, 1999).

Demos, John Putnam. *Entertaining Satan: Witchcraft and the Culture of Early New England* (New York: Oxford University Press, 1982); abbreviated in the "Notes" as *ES*.

Gildrie, Richard. *Salem, Massachusetts, 1626–1683: A Covenanted Community* (Charlottesville: University of Virginia, 1975).

Godbeer, Richard. *The Devil's Dominion: Magic and Religion in Early New England* (New York: Cambridge University Press, 1992); abbreviated in the "Notes" as *DD*.

Gragg, Larry. *A Quest for Security: The Life of Samuel Parris, 1653-1720* (Westport, CT: Greenwood Press, 1990).

——. *The Salem Witch Crisis* (New York: Praeger, 1992); abbreviated in the text as *SWC*.

Green, Rayna, and Melanie Fernandez. *The British Museum Encyclopedia of Native North America* (Bloomington, IN: Indiana University Press, 1999).

Hall, David D. *Worlds of Wonder, Days of Judgment: Popular Religious Belief in Early New England* (New York: Knopf, 1989); abbreviated in the "Notes" as *WW*.

——, ed. *Witch-Hunting in Seventeenth-Century New England: A*

Documentary History, 1638 (Boston: Northeast University Press, 1993; rev. ed., 1999) (page citations are to the 1999 edition); abbreviated in the "Notes" as *WH*.

Hambrick-Stowe, Charles E. *The Practice of Piety: Puritan Devotional Practices in Seventeenth-Century New England* (Chapel Hill, NC: University of North Carolina Press, 1982).

Hansen, Chadwick. "The Metamorphosis of Tituba: Or, Why American Intellectuals Can't Tell an Indian Witch from a Negro." *New England Quarterly*, vol. 47, no. 1 (March 1974): 3–12.

——. *Witchcraft at Salem* (New York: Brazillier, 1969).

Hawthorne, Nathaniel. "Endicott and the Red Cross." In *Twice-Told Tales* (New York: Modern Library, 2001).

Heyrman, Christine Leigh. *Commerce and Culture: The Maritime Communities of Colonial Massachusetts, 1960–1750* (New York: Norton, 1984); abbreviated in the "Notes" as *CC*.

Hill, Frances. *A Delusion of Satan: The Full Story of the Salem Witch Trials* (New York: Da Capo Press, 1997).

Hoffer, Peter Charles. *The Salem Witchcraft Trials: A Legal History* (Lawrence: University Press of Kansas, 1997).

Kamensky, Jane. *Governing the Tongue: The Politics of Speech in Early New England* (New York: Oxford University Press, 1997).

Karlsen, Carl. *The Devil in the Shape of a Woman: Witchcraft in Colonial New England* (New York: Norton, 1987; reprinted, 1998) (page citations are to the 1998 reprint edition).

Konig, David Thomas. *Law and Society in Puritan Massachusetts: Essex County, 1629–1692* (Chapel Hill, NC: University of North Carolina Press, 1979).

Le Beau, Bryan F. *The Story of the Salem Witch Trials* (Upper Saddle River, NJ: Prentice-Hall, 1998); abbreviated in the "Notes" as *SWT.*

Miller, Arthur. *Timebends* (New York: Grove Press, 1989).

———. *The Crucible* (New York: Viking Press, 1953).

Morgan, Edmund. *Visible Saints: The History of a Puritan Idea* (Ithaca, NY: Cornell University Press, 1963).

Norton, Mary Beth. "Finding the Devil in the Details of the Salem Witchcraft Trials." *Chronicle of Higher Education,* (January 21, 2000).

———. *In the Devil's Snare: The Salem Witchcraft Crisis of 1692* (New York: Knopf, 2002); abbreviated in the "Notes" as *DS.*

Perley, Sidney. *The History of Salem, Massachusetts,* vol. 3, *1671–1716* (Salem, MA: Sidney Perley, 1928).

Phillips, James Duncan. *Salem in the Eighteenth Century* (Boston: Houghton Mifflin, 1937).

Roach, Marilynne K. *The Salem Witch Trials: A Day-by-Day Chronicle of a Community Under Siege.* (New York: Cooper Square Press, 2002).

Rosenthal, Bernard. *Salem Story: Reading the Witch Trials of 1692* (Cambridge, England: Cambridge University Press, 1993); abbreviated in the "Notes" as *SS*.

Starkey, Marion. *The Devil in Massachusetts* (New York: Knopf, 1950).

Thomas, Keith. *Religion and the Decline of Magic* (Oxford, England: Oxford University Press, 1971).

Upham, Charles W. *Salem Witchcraft: With an Account of Salem Village and a History of Opinions on Witchcraft and Kindred Spirits.* 2 vols. (1867; reprint, New York: Frederick Ungar Publishing, 1966); abbreviated in the "Notes" as *SW*.

Weisman, Richard. *Witchcraft, Magic, and Religion in 17th-Century Massachusetts* (Amherst: University of Massachusetts Press, 1984).

Williams, Selma, and Pamela Williams Adelman. *Riding the Nightmare: Women and Witchcraft from the Old World to Colonial Salem.* (New York: HarperCollins, 1978; reprint, New York: HarperPerennial, 1991) (page citations are to the 1991 edition).

Index

S

Salem

    splitting of, 48–49, 52–53, 120, 200

    tensions in, 200, 212

Salem Possessed (Boyer and Nissenbaum), 212

Salem Story (Rosenthal), 214

Salem Town, 48, 52–53, 120

Salem Village, 49, 50, 52, 120, 122

Salem Witchcraft (Upham), 210

Salem Witchcraft Papers (Boyer and Nissenbaum), 212

Salem Witchcraft Trials, The (Hoffer), 215

Salem Witch Crisis, The (Gragg), 218

Saltonstall, Nathaniel, 131–132, 138, 165, 182

salvation, 44–45

September 11, 2001, 219, 221

Sewall, Samuel, 44–45, 126, 130, 131, 148, 151, 184, 186–187

Sheldon, Susannah, 4, 5, 111, 112–113

Sibley, Mary, 66, 67, 71

skeptics, 132–133, 136, 138, 166, 181–182

Sleeping Beauty, 9–10, 11

spectral evidence, 133, 137, 184

Starkey, Marion, 210, 221

Stoughton, William, 131, 136, 138, 148, 161, 170, 181–184

T

terror, war against, 226–227

tests

    of church members, 46

    of witches, 17, 66, 96–97, 105, 135, 163